WYVERN COLLECTION
OBJECTS IN FOCUS

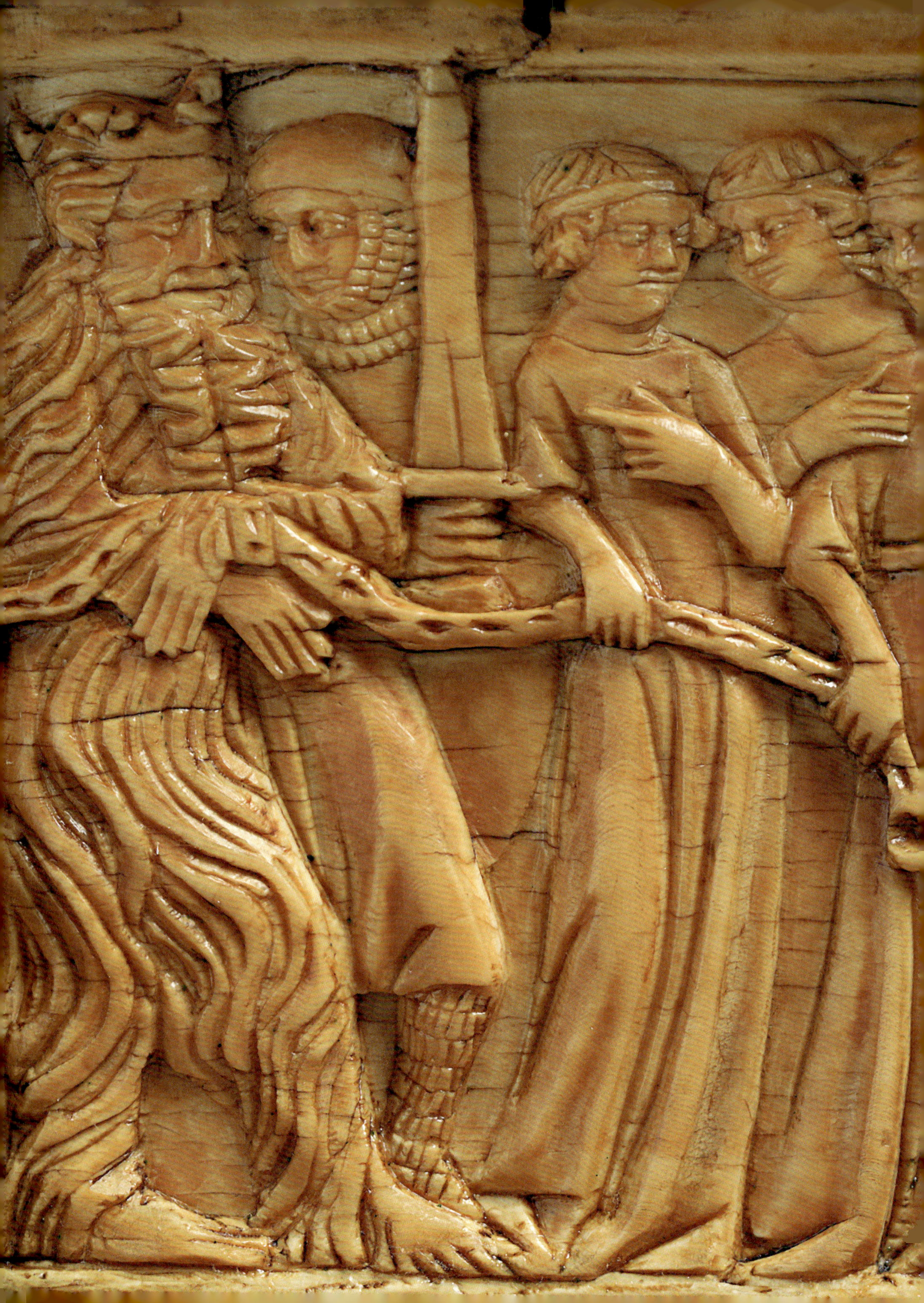

WYVERN COLLECTION
OBJECTS IN FOCUS

Volume I

The Baird Casket

Paul Williamson

AD ILISSVM

WYVERN COLLECTION
OBJECTS IN FOCUS

This book is the first in a series produced by the Wyvern Research Institute devoted to the in-depth analysis of a single object, or small group of objects, in the Wyvern Collection. Combining art historical research with technical analysis, the series captures the Institute's mission to stimulate new lines of investigation and disseminate fresh critical insights to a broad audience.

The Wyvern Research Institute is a centre for advanced research in the history of art, with a focus on the Byzantine and Medieval periods as well as the Silk Roads. It is associated with the Wyvern Collection, one of the world's most significant private collections, which encompasses over two thousand objects dating from as early as the fourth millennium BC to the nineteenth century, traversing broad geographic boundaries across a range of media. The Wyvern Research Institute's mission is to support the research and teaching of art history, with a focus on object centred study.

CONTENTS

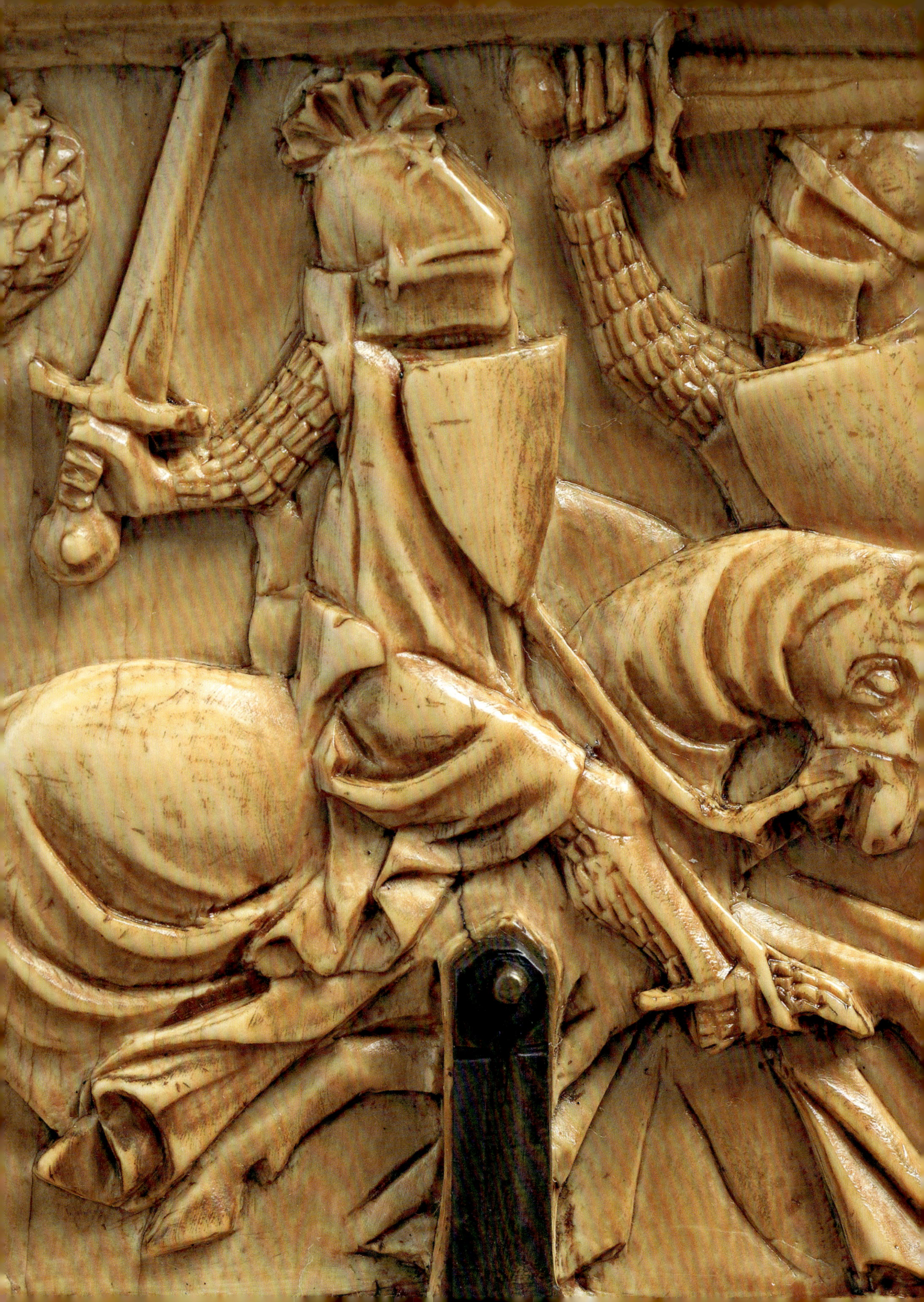

ACKNOWLEDGEMENTS

I am most grateful to Dr Alison Stones, Professor Emerita at the University of Pittsburgh, and Dr Martine Meuwese of the University of Utrecht, for so freely sharing their deep knowledge of Arthurian and Grail imagery with me, and for their invaluable comments on the text – although they are not responsible for my conclusions. I also have to thank Michaela Zöschg, of the Victoria and Albert Museum, for kindly reading the essay and offering several pertinent observations. Susannah Kingwill, the Director of the Wyvern Research Institute, has been supportive throughout, especially in the procurement of the images; and for the production of the publication I have to thank Paul Holberton, the editor, and Laura Parker, who has laid it out with sensitivity and flair. It is a pleasure once again to thank the owner of the Wyvern Collection, who invited me to write this monograph.

PAUL WILLIAMSON

THE BAIRD CASKET

Introduction

Occasionally, completely unknown works of art of the first importance appear without warning on the art market. While it is not often the case that these discoveries match the overwhelming significance of such archaeological or chance finds as the Anglo-Saxon Sutton Hoo Ship Burial and the Staffordshire Hoard, or the Late Antique Mildenhall Treasure (all three of which necessitated the rewriting of accepted histories), some of them nevertheless add striking new evidence to their fields of study.

It continues to surprise even specialists that objects of the highest quality are still emerging well into the twenty-first century, sometimes through dealers and sporadically at auction, from private collections in Britain where they have rested undisturbed, unheralded and unpublished for decades or even centuries. Such was the case with the extremely rare and splendid ivory mirror case, in pristine condition and with both discs extant, which entered the Wyvern Collection in September 2018 (fig. 1). Until then, this finest of Gothic ivories had lain unnoticed in a drawer at Lulworth Castle in Dorset, in the Weld Collection, and was only brought to the attention of Sotheby's in the year before its acquisition for the Wyvern Collection.[1]

An equally astonishing discovery is the subject of this short monograph, an intriguing and singular Gothic ivory casket showing scenes of combat with wild men and their capture, adorned with carvings celebrating the power of the sword, culminating in its presence at the Round Table (plate 1). The images, some not previously recorded on Gothic ivories, are unusual in themselves – and even more so in combination – but the interest of the object is increased further by its fascinating post-medieval history.

The casket was unknown to the public until shortly before its sale at the Edinburgh premises of the auctioneers Lyon & Turnbull on 20 May 2021.[2] It was revealed in the catalogue that the casket had been consigned by descendants of the Baird family, and that it had been kept at Tornaveen House in Aberdeenshire. Furthermore, documentary evidence was brought forward to establish its earlier ownership by the Bairds of Auchmedden, certainly by the eighteenth century and possibly as early as the first half of the seventeenth century. The key text here is William Nathaniel Fraser's edited volume, the *Account of the Surname of Baird, particularly of the families of Auchmedden, Newbyth and Sauchtonhall*, published in two editions in 1857 and 1870.[3] Fraser

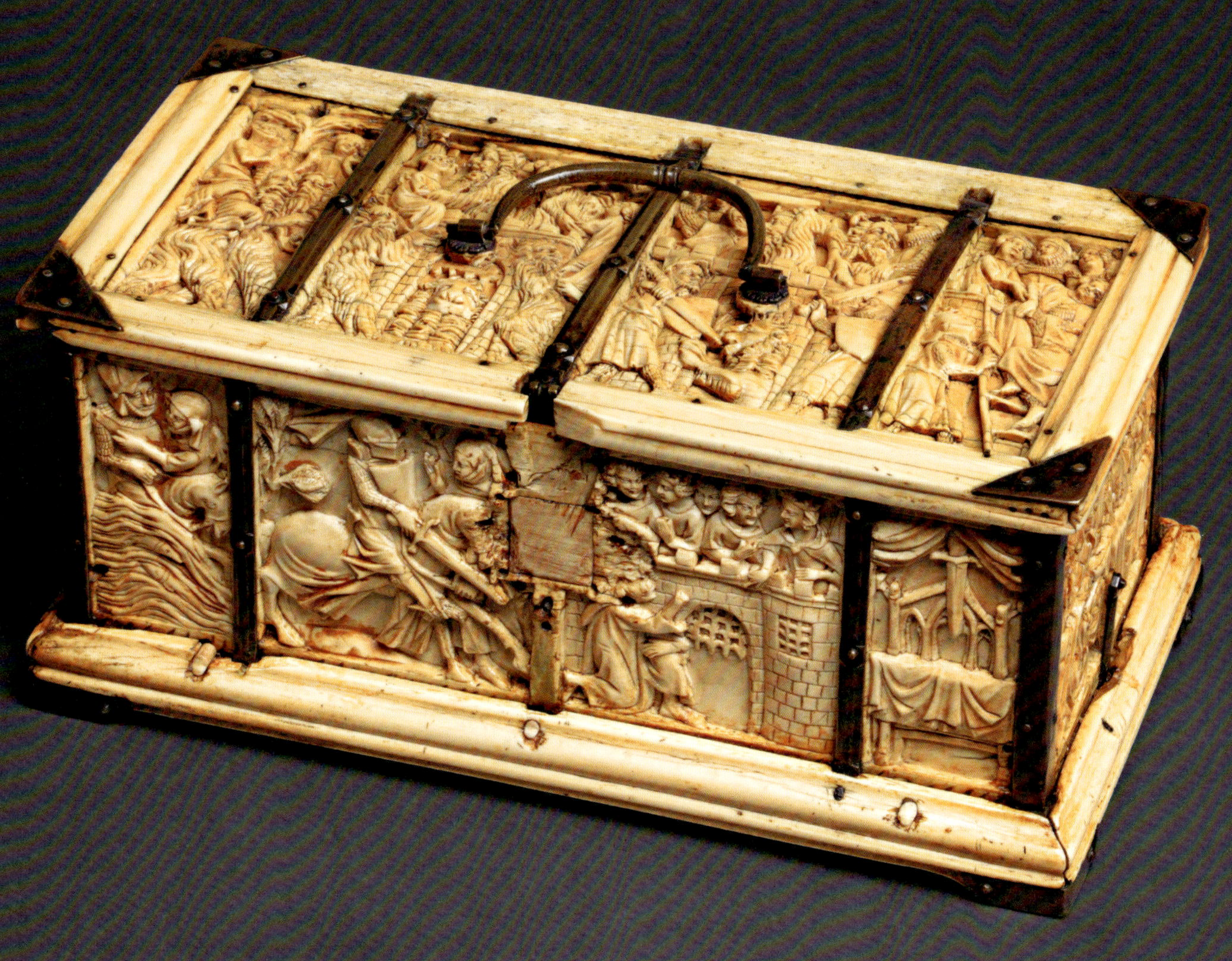

PLATE 1

The Baird casket, general view with scenes of
Lancelot (?), the Grail Legend and wild men. Paris or
Flanders (?), c. 1320–30, with additions of c. 1430–70

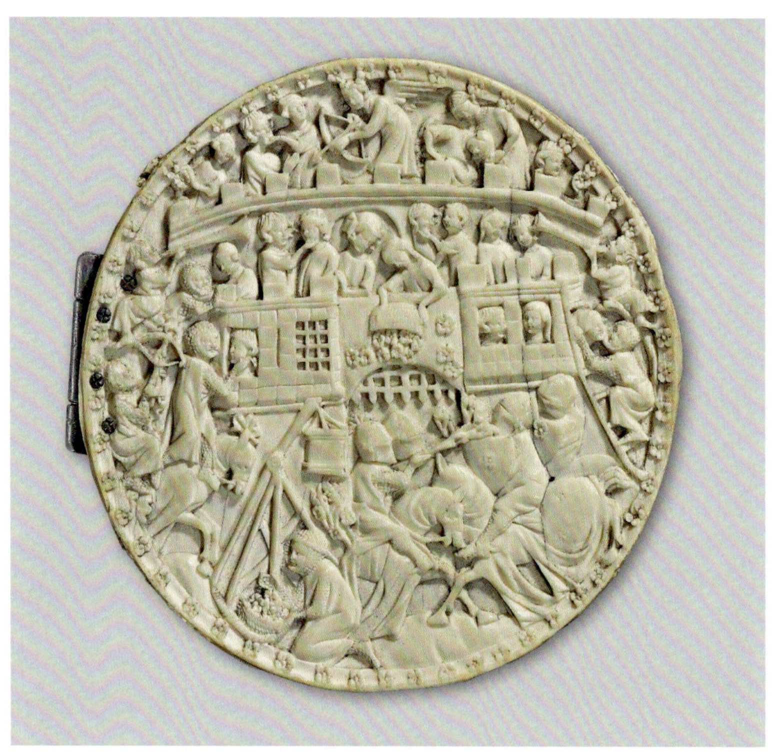

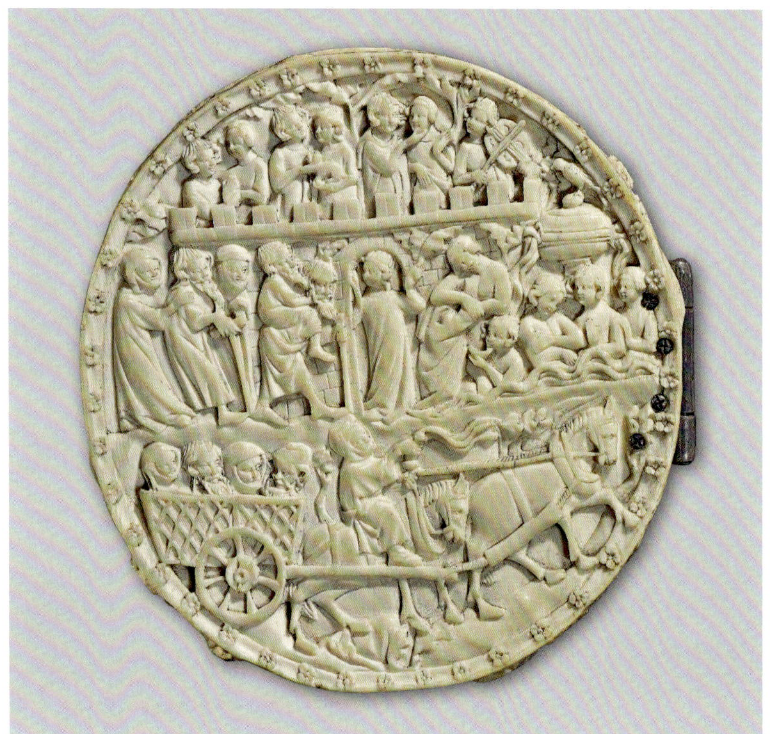

1. Mirror case with the Fountain of Youth and the
Storming of the Castle of Love, French (Paris),
c. 1300–20 (Wyvern Collection, London)

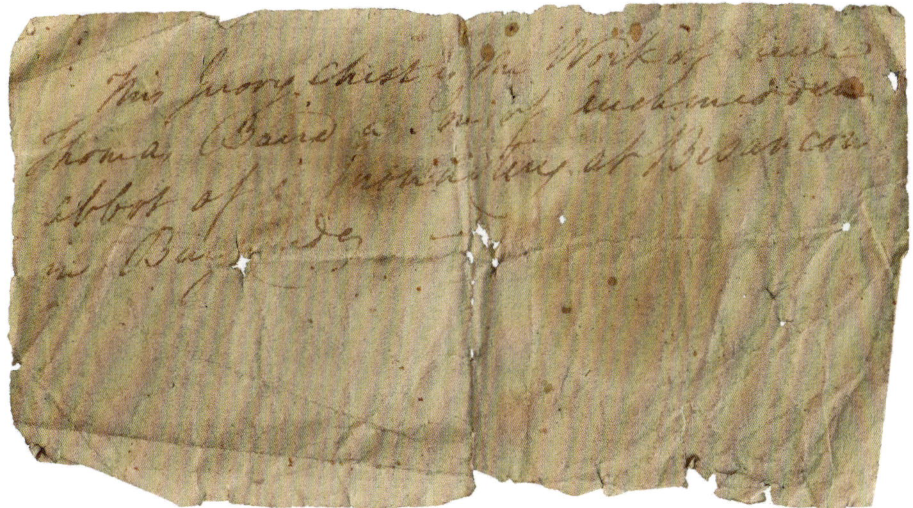

2. Label from inside the Baird casket

pointed out in the preface to the book that the 'genealogy of the family of Baird has been printed here for the first time from a manuscript written by William Baird, Esquire, of Auchmedden, the last male representative [of the Baird family]'.[4] It is to William Baird (c. 1701–1777) that we owe the only mention of the casket, when he ascribes it, without proof and clearly erroneously, to the efforts of his ancestor Thomas Baird (d. 1649): '[...] he had an excellent turn to mechanics, of which a very good sample is still to be seen. It is an oblong, small chest of Ivory 10 inches [25.5 cm] long, 5 [13 cm] broad, and 4 [10 cm] high, delicately carved in bas-relief, with the chisel upon the top and sides into figures of knight-errants, distrest damsels, and enchanted castles, taken from some of the old romances which were so much in vogue in that age.'[5] At the time of the 2021 sale there was a paper slip inside the casket (fig. 2) with an inscription written in ink in an eighteenth-century hand: 'This Ivory Chest is the Work of deceased / Thomas Baird a son of Auchmedden / abbot of a monastery at Besancon / in Burgundy'.[6] It is possible that William Baird based his attribution of the casket to Thomas Baird on this testimony.

The seventeenth-century letters assembled by William Baird give a partial account of Thomas Baird's life, even though they make no mention of the casket. At a very young age, in 1607, he was sent from Scotland to stay with his uncle Andrew Baird, a former professor of philosophy at Lyon and by then a minim friar at Besançon, and he had settled there by 1609.[7] In 1615 he had himself become a minim friar at Besançon, and in the same year his uncle wrote to Thomas's father, Gilbert Baird, that 'when I shall go to Flanders I will bring him with me'.[8] Two years later, on 12 October 1617, Andrew Baird wrote again to Gilbert Baird, frankly disclosing Thomas's character and capabilities:

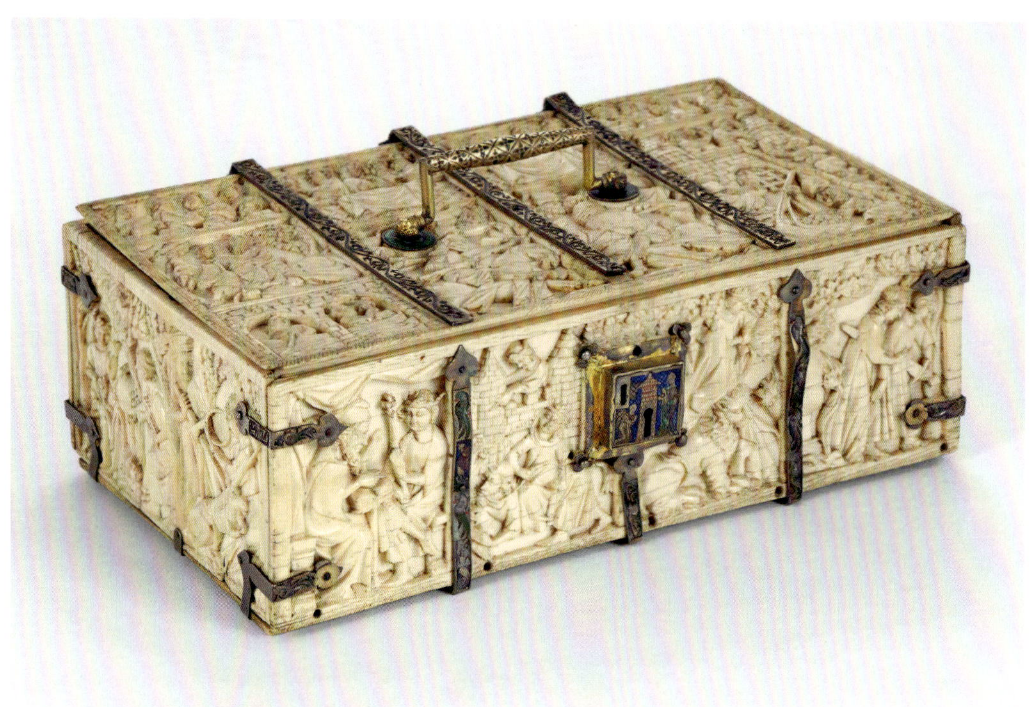

3. Composite casket, French (Paris), c. 1300–20
(Wawel Royal Cathedral, Cracow)

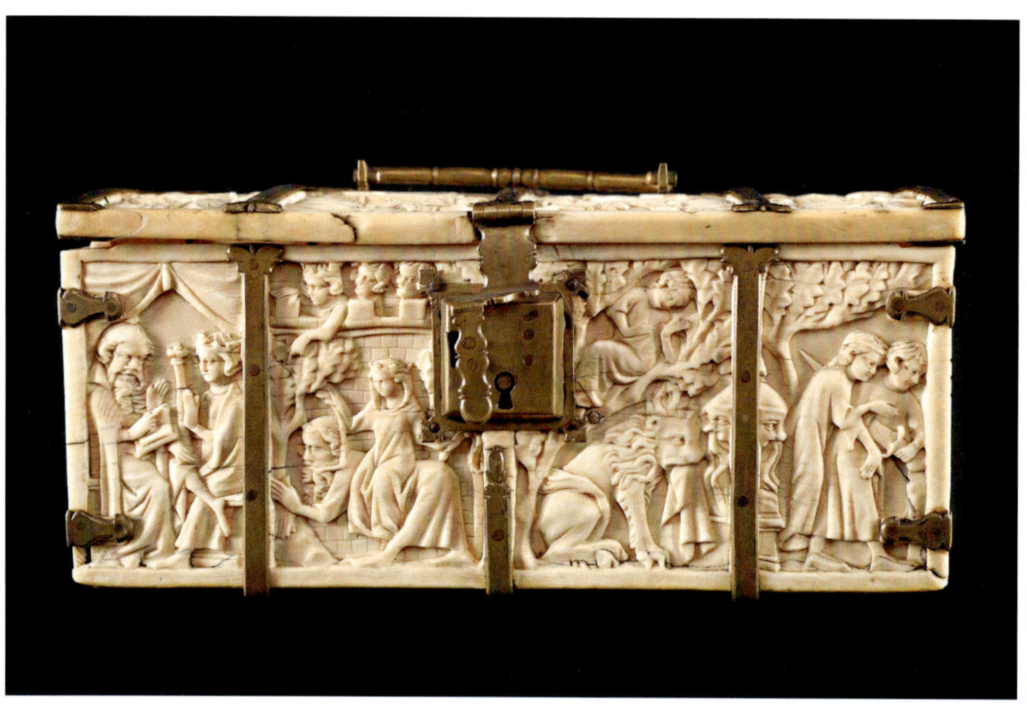

4. Composite casket, French (Paris), c. 1310–30
(Barber Institute of Fine Arts, Birmingham)

'Thomas, [...] a good boy, serviceable, but is not of great wit nor turn to letters. He has a very hard *ingyne* [lack of natural intelligence] and is no great scholar, but I houp he sall be a guid man. He speaks very good Frenshe, but he writte not well.'[9] In 1632 both Thomas and his uncle were both still 'in lyfe and weil', but no more is heard of Thomas before his death in 1649.[10]

So, in reality there is nothing to link the casket to Thomas Baird in the letters, and we have to rely entirely on William Baird's statement, probably from the 1770s, and the label once inside the casket, for this connection. Given the inherent unlikeliness of the casket being the work of a craftsman in the early seventeenth century, much less an untrained Scottish friar, one can only surmise that the legend passed on by William Baird was simply family folklore. All we can say is that the casket seems to have been in the possession of the Bairds long before the middle of the eighteenth century, and it is quite possible – even probable – that it made its way to Auchmedden as part of the modest chattels of Thomas Baird, or maybe those of Andrew Baird, after their deaths. It seems appropriate, therefore, to call it the 'Baird casket', and in the first two scholarly discussions of the object it has indeed been labelled as such.[11]

As we have seen, by 1857 the casket had passed to W.N. Fraser, and remained with his descendants until its sale in 2021.[12] It was bought at the Lyon & Turnbull auction by a Canadian private collector, who in turn sold it through Sam Fogg in London to the Wyvern Collection in June 2024.[13]

The history of most Gothic ivory carvings can rarely be traced back before the middle of the nineteenth century, so that those with a firm provenance before 1800 are particularly important when it comes to the history of collecting and even questions of authenticity.[14] Only a very few fourteenth-century ivory caskets comparable to the present example fall into this category. Three of these, in Cracow, Birmingham and Baltimore, are of the type known as 'composite' caskets (*coffrets composites*), and are covered with various scenes of chivalry and romance.[15] That in the cathedral treasury of Cracow (fig. 3) – romantically known as 'Queen Jadwiga's casket' – was itemized in an inventory of 1563; the casket in the Barber Institute of Fine Arts at the University of Birmingham (fig. 4), according to the late nineteenth-century ink inscription on a label stuck to the inside of the lid, was owned by Francis Annesley, 1st Viscount Valentia (1585–1660); and the casket now in the Walters Art Museum in Baltimore (fig. 5) had belonged to Francis Douce (1757–1834) before 1803, and was previously in the possession of the eighteenth-century antiquaries the Revd John Bowle and Gustavus Brander (d. 1787).[16]

The other surviving composite caskets are now kept in the Victoria and Albert Museum (fig. 6), the British Museum (fig. 7), the Metropolitan Museum of Art in New York (fig. 8), the Museo Nazionale del Bargello in Florence (fig. 9) and the Musée de Cluny in Paris (fig. 10). Most of these do not have

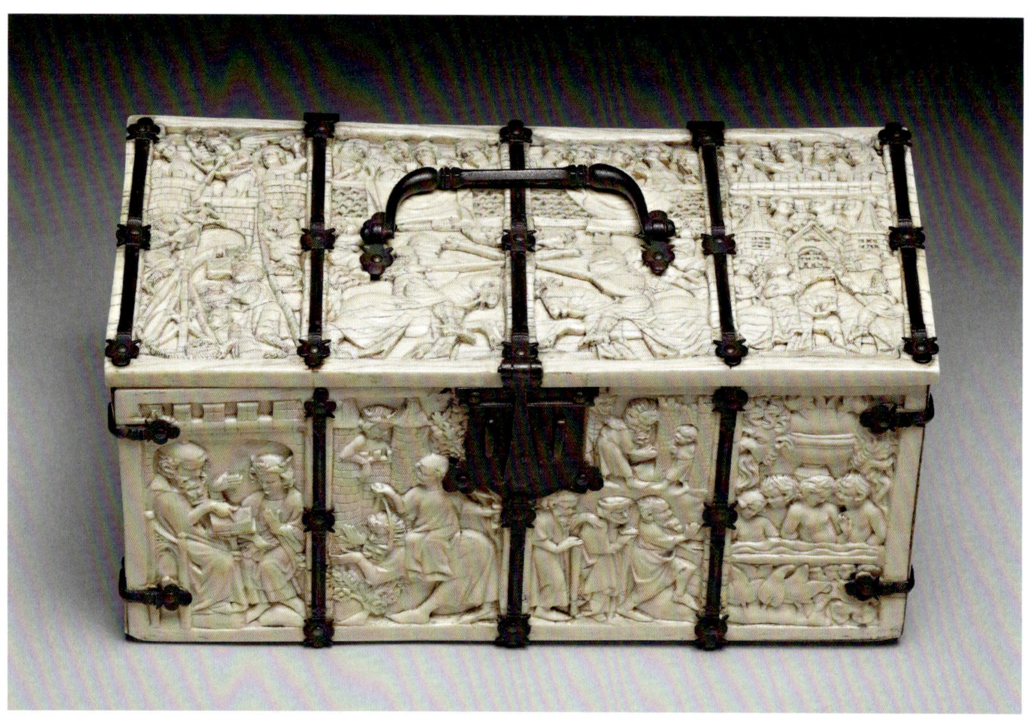

5. Composite casket, French (Paris), c. 1310–30
(Walters Art Museum, Baltimore)

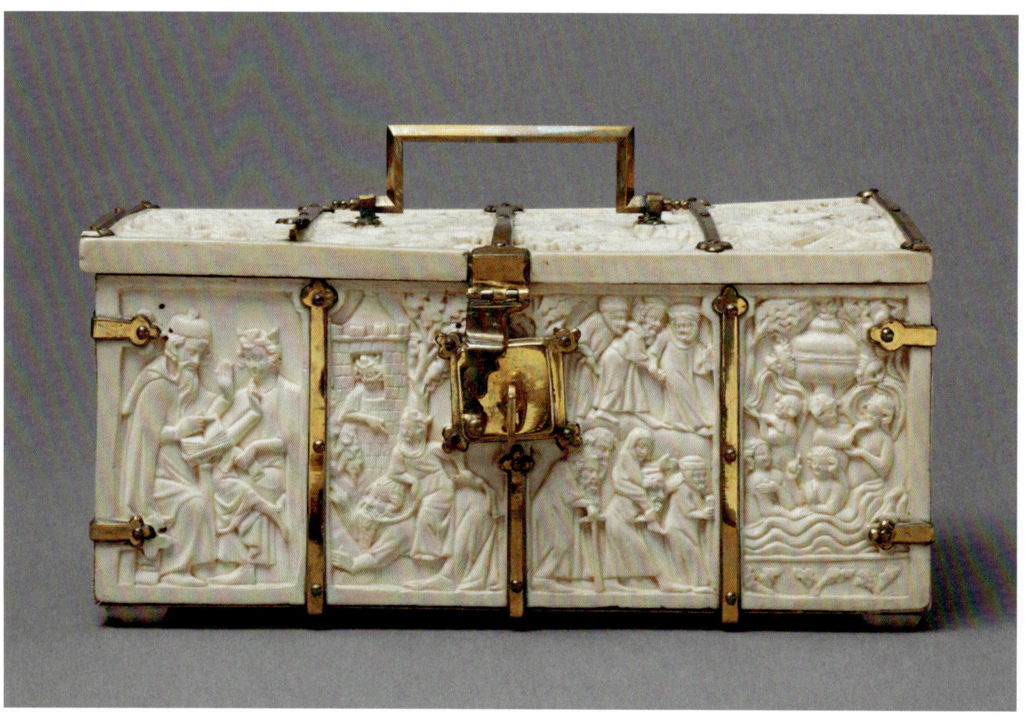

6. Composite casket, French (Paris), c. 1310–30
(Victoria and Albert Museum, London)

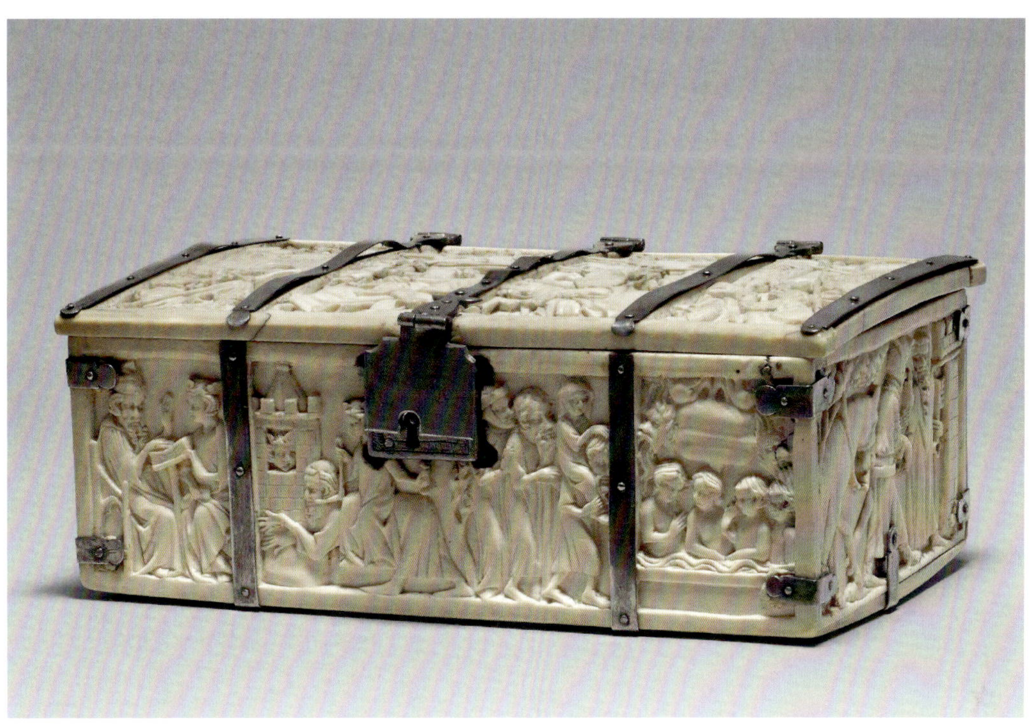

7. Composite casket, French (Paris), c. 1310–30
(British Museum, London)

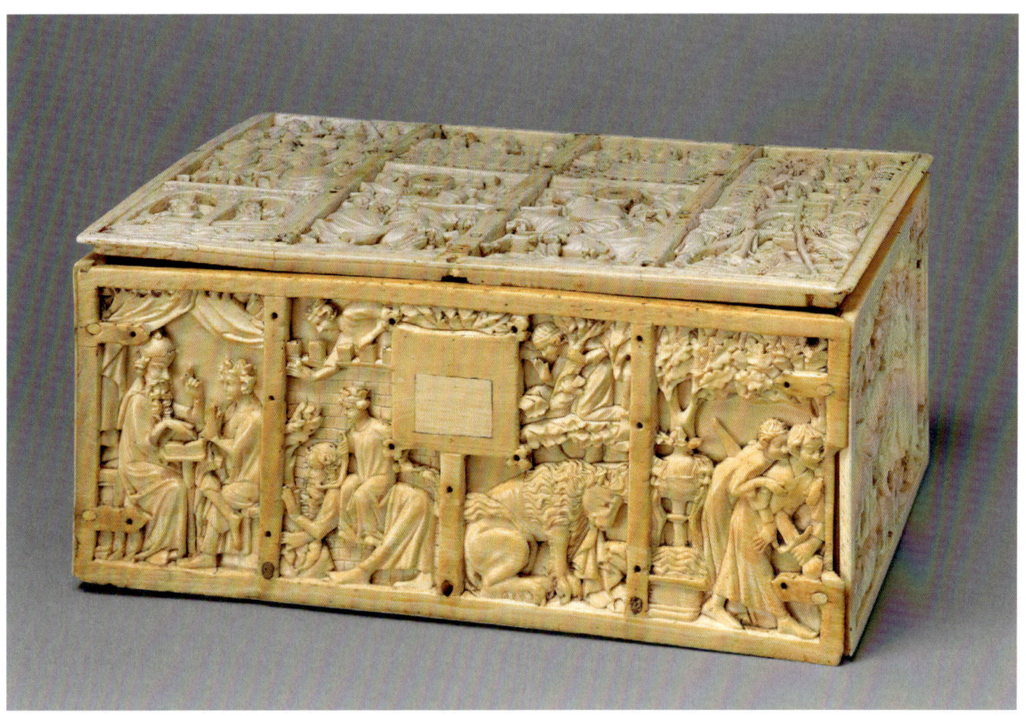

8. Composite casket, French (Paris), c. 1310–30
(Metropolitan Museum of Art, The Cloisters, New York)

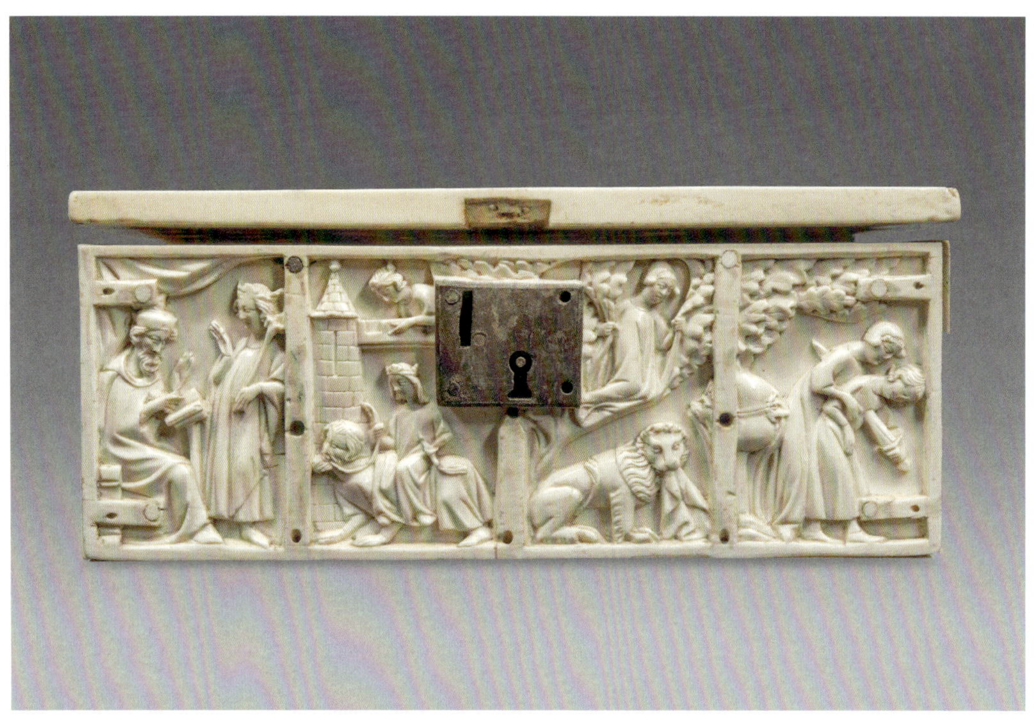

9. Composite casket, French (Paris), c. 1310–30
(Museo Nazionale del Bargello, Florence)

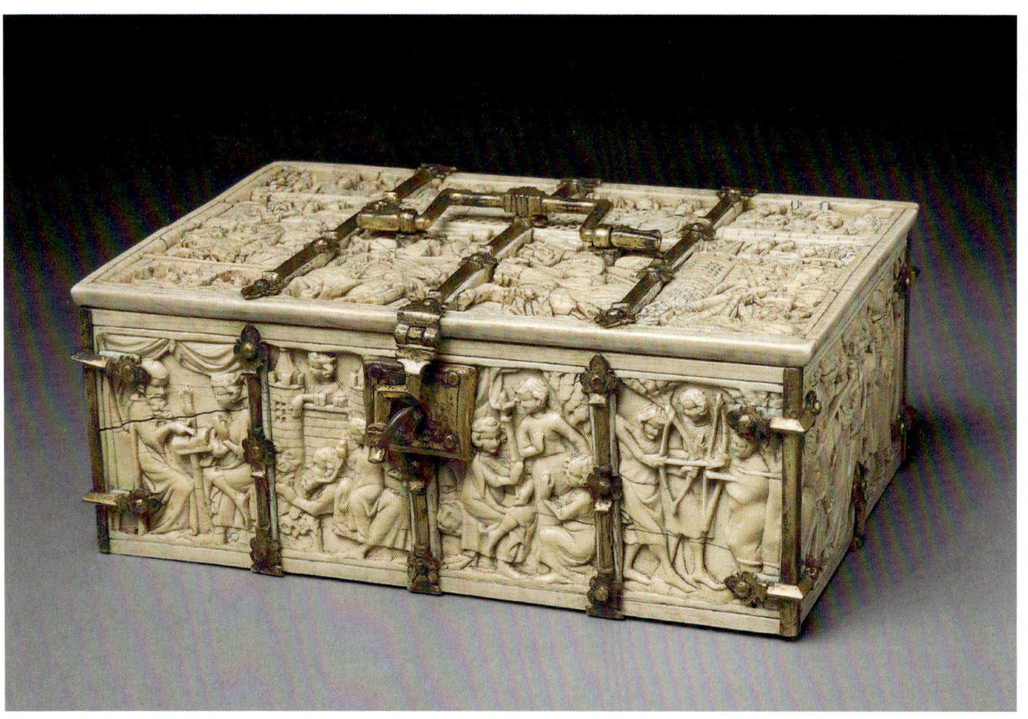

10. Composite casket, French (Paris), c. 1300–20
(Musée de Cluny, Paris)

a provenance that can be traced back much before the middle of the nineteenth century. The eight composite caskets are clearly a coherent group, in both their subject matter and style, and there is now scholarly consensus that they were carved in a Parisian workshop (or workshops), probably in the years 1300–30.[17] The Baird casket, on the other hand, although also a composite casket in its compilation of scenes drawn from various sources, clearly stands apart in its subject matter, and the iconographical peculiarities found on its carved panels possibly point to a different place of production.

A Description of the Casket and its Imagery

FACTURE

The casket is made up of five principal plaques of ivory, on to which the narrative scenes are carved on the front faces, and a base plate of ivory.[18] The backs of the plaques, on the inside of the casket, would originally have been covered with cloth, and have numerous lines incised into the surface to act as a ground for adhesive.[19] The vertical plaques are joined together at the corners with lap joints (plate 2), as was customary with the composite and other caskets of the fourteenth century, and the structural stability of the box is reinforced by the application of three flat-sectioned, faceted copper-alloy (probably brass) strips fixed with three round-headed nails on the front, back and lid; there are single short mounts on the side panels. All the metal mounts on the vertical walls of the casket, which are set against flat uncarved strips, are fixed at right angles on the underside of the base (fig. 11). These mounts might not be original, and the plain mounts of L-section at the corners are certainly of later date, replacing the two now-missing small mounts that wrapped round the long and short sides; the holes for these are still visible near the corners, and all the complete composite caskets illustrate these elements.[20] The majority of the caskets also show how the now-missing lock plate and clasp of the Baird casket would have functioned.[21]

The composite caskets additionally give a clear impression of the original appearance and proportions of the Baird casket before it was radically transformed by the addition of the moulded base and the frame of the lid. The main body of the casket, with the narrative scenes, can be dated with confidence to the first half of the fourteenth century, not far removed from the composite caskets group; and a more detailed analysis of the date and place of production will follow below. The base, with integrally carved stepped feet at the corners, and the moulded ivory and bone frame of the lid, however, must have been added over a century later. They are entirely consistent with those found on the ivory and bone caskets now associated with workshops in the Southern

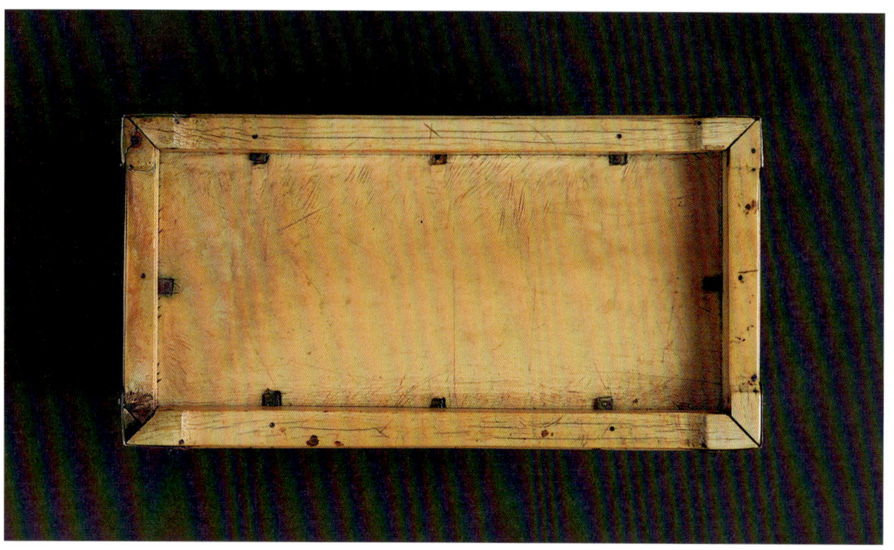

11. The underside of the casket

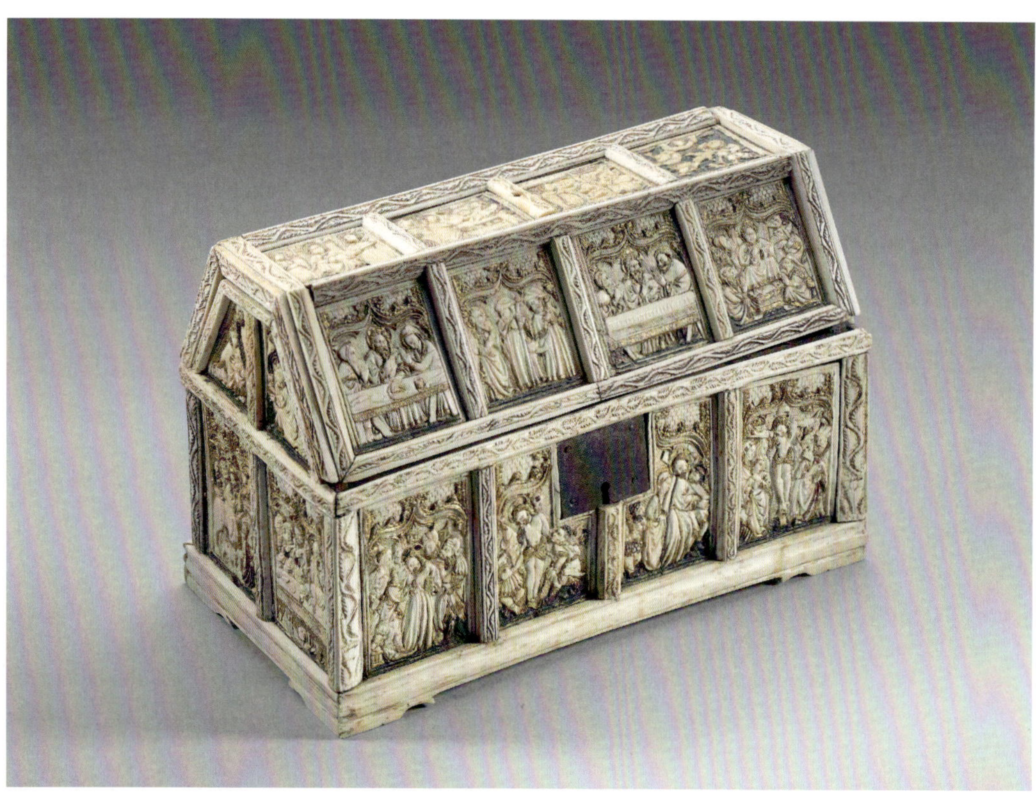

12. Casket with scenes from the Life of Christ,
South Netherlandish (Flanders), c. 1430–60
(Wyvern Collection, London)

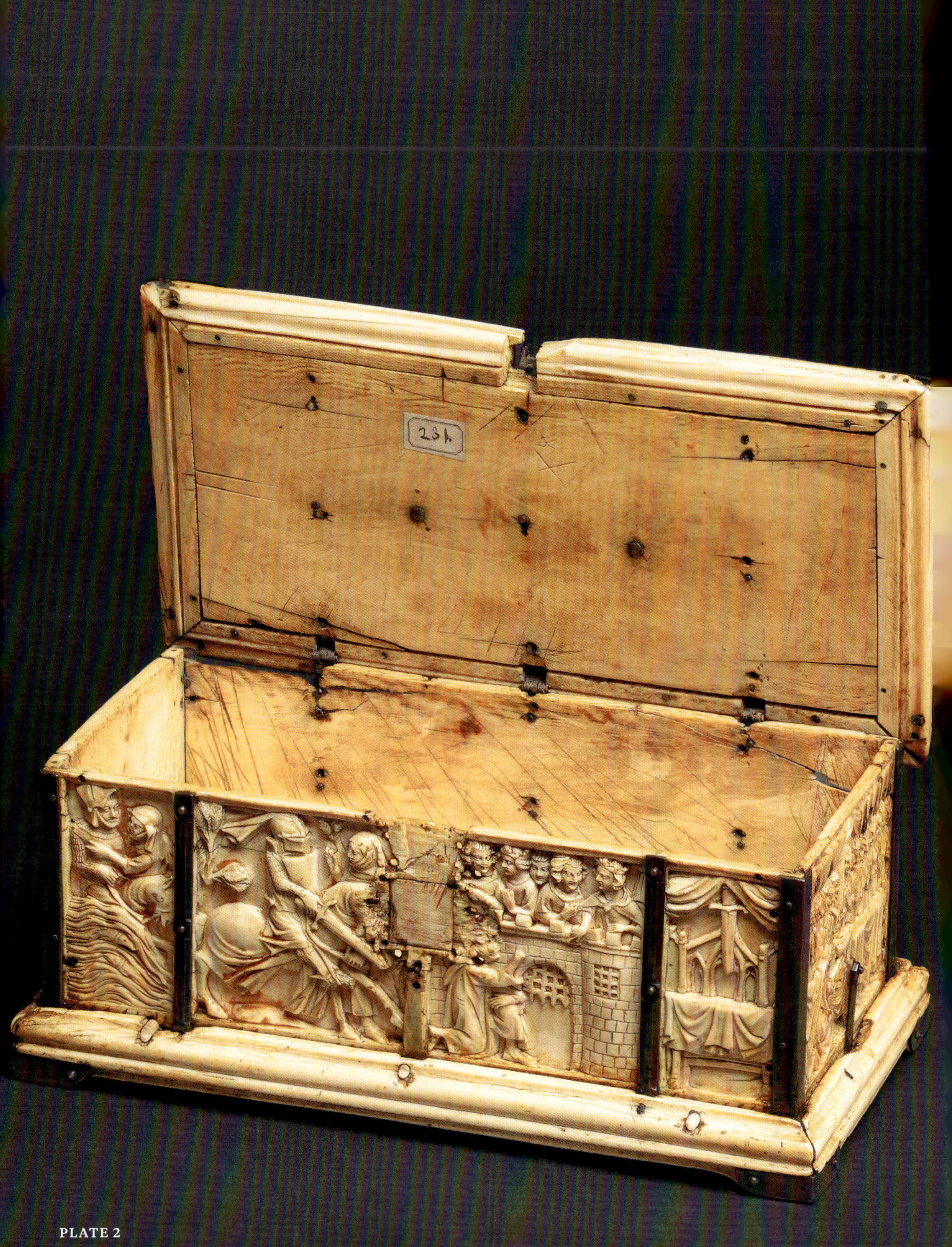

PLATE 2
The casket with lid open

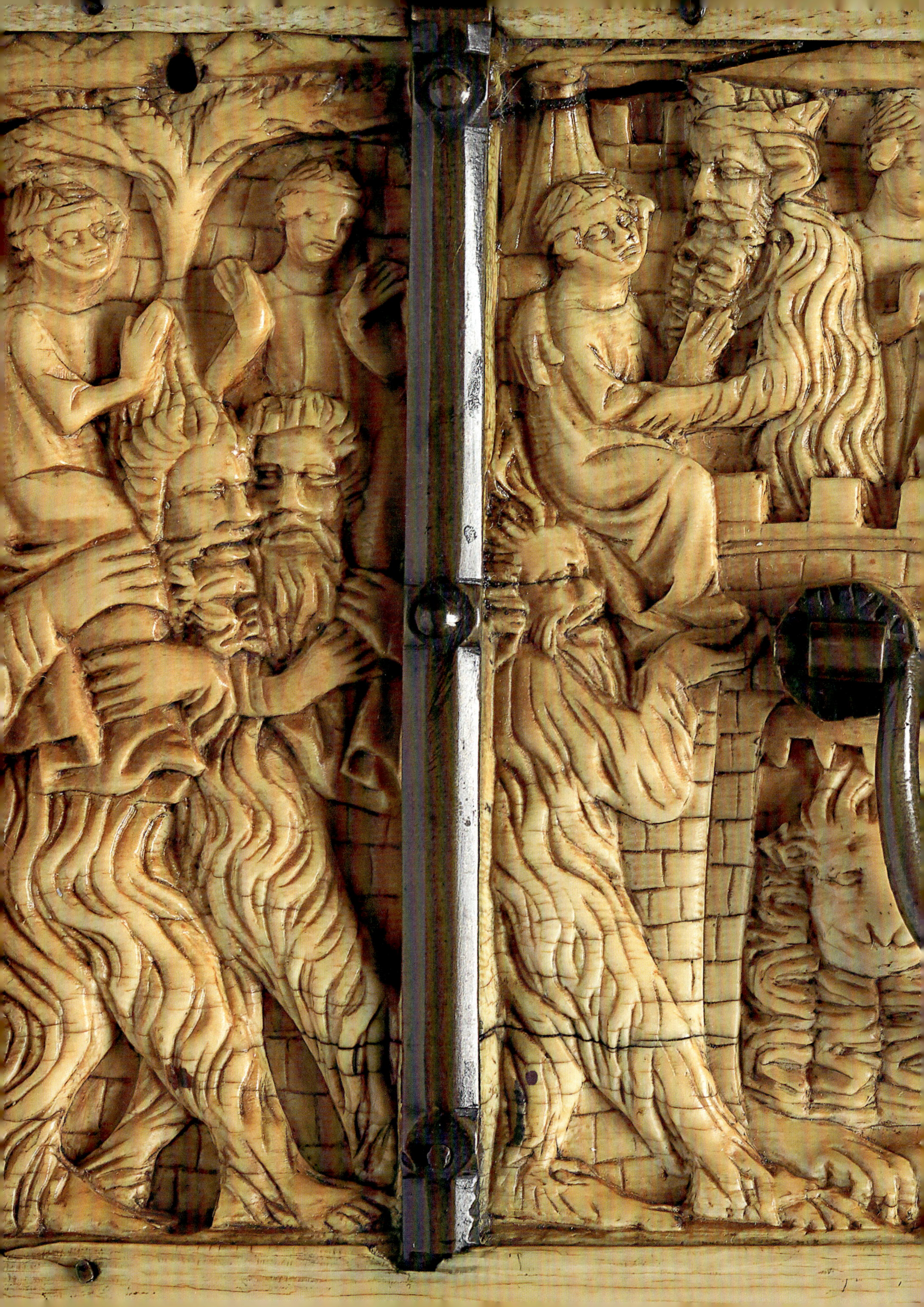

Netherlands and dated *c.* 1430–70; an example in the Wyvern Collection displays just such a base (fig. 12).[22] So it would seem that the casket was in the area of Flanders by the middle of the fifteenth century, where it was restored, perhaps following some damage that threatened its structural solidity.[23]

At the same time that the base and the moulded frame of the lid were added, the L-sectioned corner mounts of the body of the casket were fitted to replace the original double clasps; these mounts are of the same metal as the triangular mounts reinforcing the corners of the lid and those covering the feet on the base. At a later, indeterminate, date the lock and its clasp were ripped from the casket (an act almost certainly connected with the theft of its contents), never to be replaced. When the lock and clasp were torn off, considerable damage was done to the surrounding surface and the frame above; apart from this, and several cracks running through some of the reliefs, the casket is in reasonably good condition.[24]

THE SCENES

The casket is essentially devoted to two principal themes: scenes showing wild men abducting maidens, with their rescue and the capture of the wild men on the lid and back panel, and enigmatic episodes of chivalry and the Grail on the front and right side of the box. At first glance it seems, however, that there is no over-riding single narrative that can be followed in any order around the walls and lid of the casket, and that the wild men and chivalric scenes could have been intended to be viewed as independent images, albeit linked to one another by the concept of dishonourable actions set against admirable behaviour.

The relief on the lid, divided into four by the three mounts, should be read from left to right (plate 3). Unlike the lids of the composite caskets, it does not show the Siege of the Castle of Love, with a tournament in front of the walls. In the first field two wild men are shown carrying two distressed maidens on their shoulders. In the next scene they lift the two ladies into their castle, where they are pulled up by two further wild men, the one on the left crowned; a third maiden, already captured, is shown between the two wild men, her hands joined in anxious prayer, and a lion fills the gateway beneath the open portcullis.[25] The third scene shows four knights storming the castle (three with swords), one attacking the lion and two above in combat with the crowned wild man and his companion. In the final scene, on the right, the fight is over and the knights help the three maidens out of the castle.

The story concludes on the back of the casket in a single scene that takes place over the four fields of the relief (plate 4). Three vanquished wild men, headed by their crowned king, are taken into captivity; they are bound at the

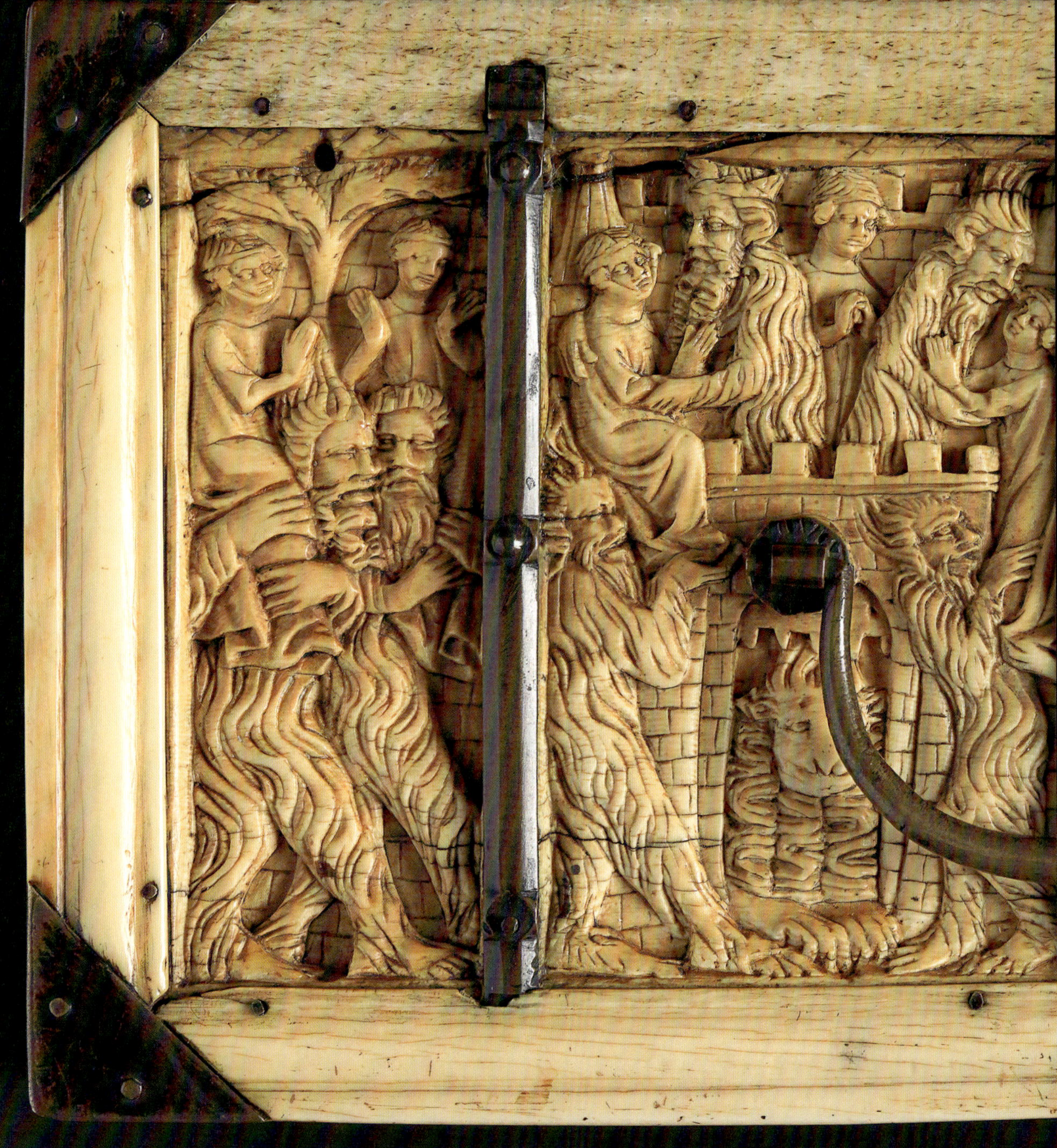

The lid of the casket, showing scenes of
combat between knights and wild men

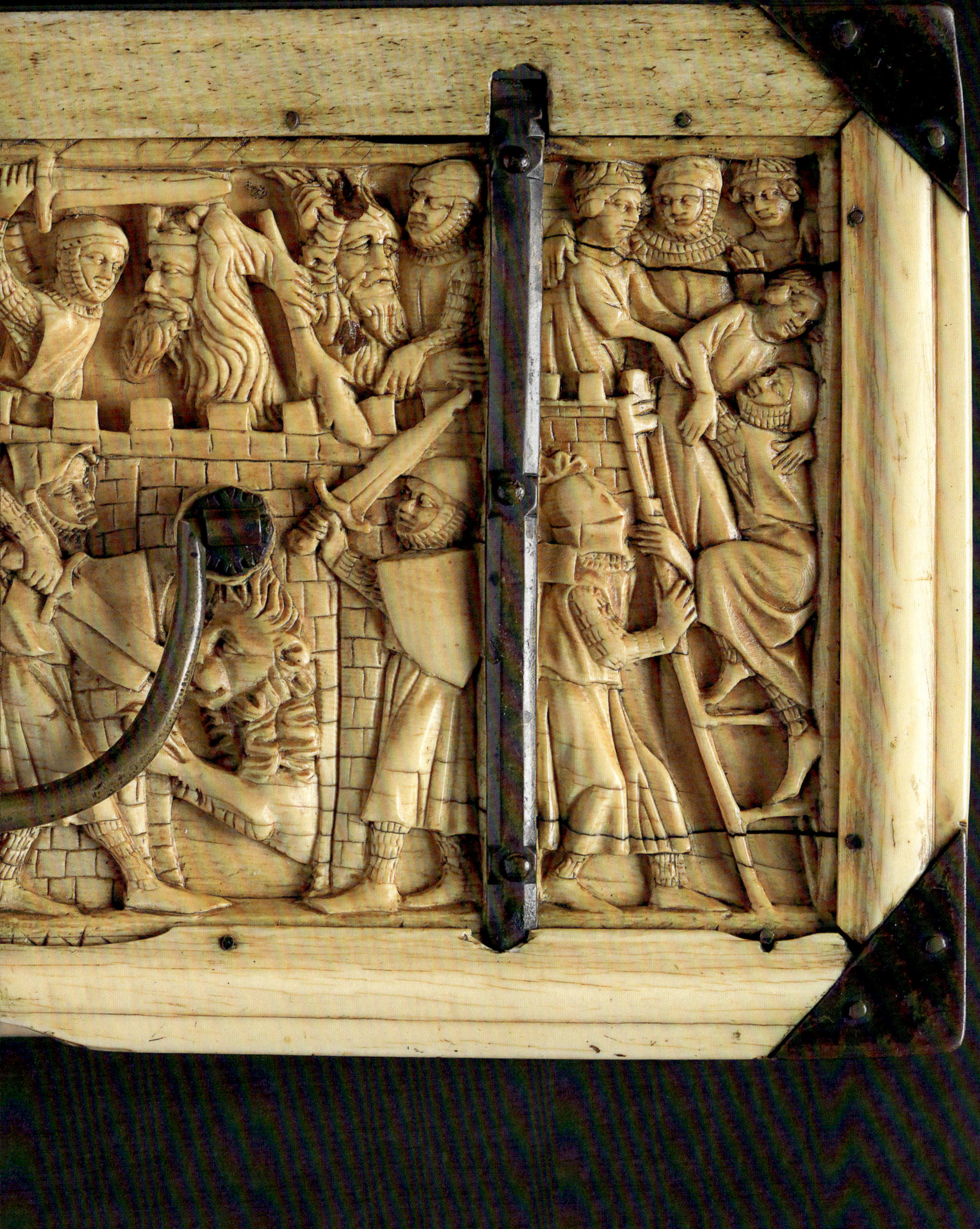

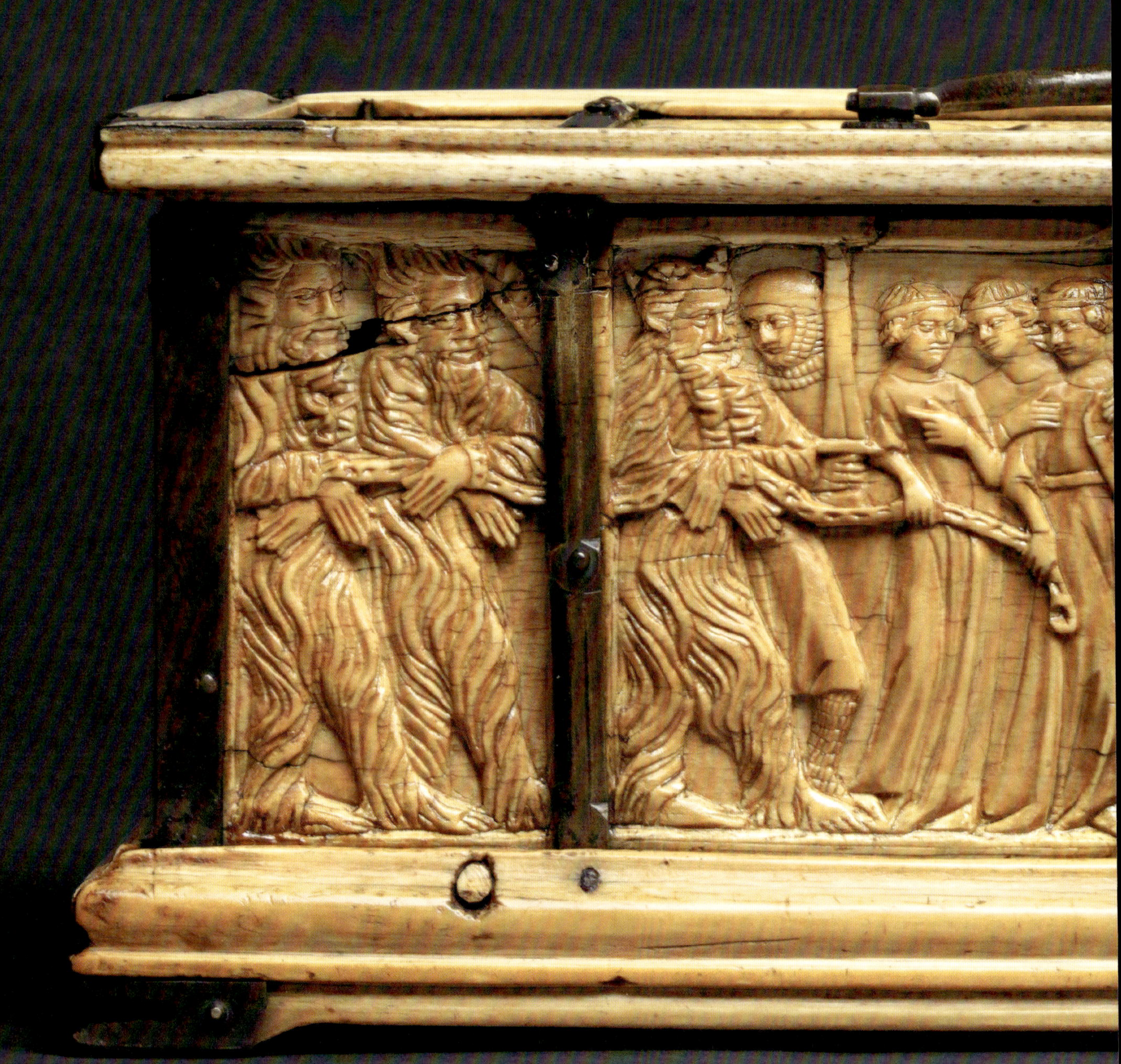

The back of the casket, showing the capture of
the wild men and their presentation to a king

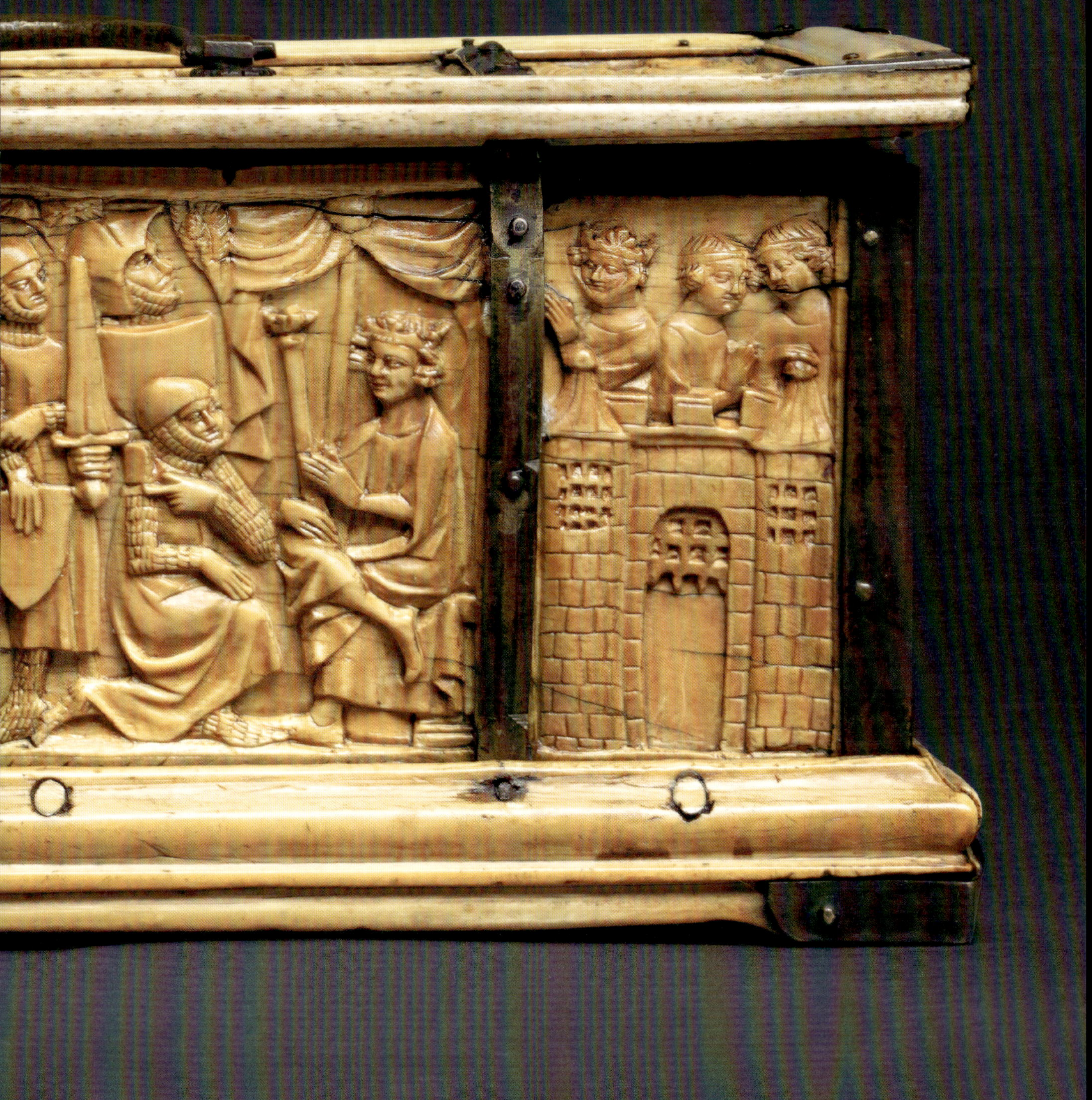

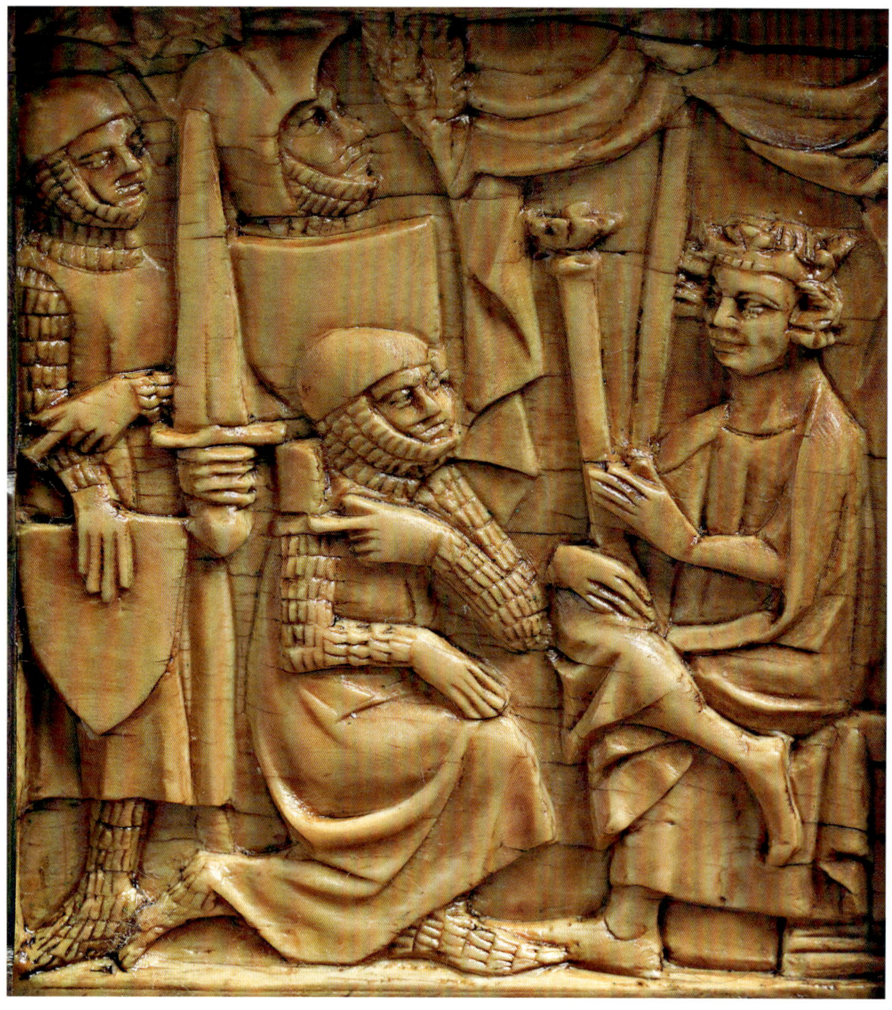

13. Detail of three knights before a king (Arthur?)
from the back of the Baird casket

wrists with a long chain and led by one of the three maidens while a sword-bearing knight looks on. The three other knights – like the three Magi before the Virgin and Child – announce the capture to the crowned king, seated within a tent, with two of them pointing back to the approaching party. Behind the king, his queen and two attendants animatedly discuss the action that is taking place before them. Comparing the figure of the king on the casket, cross-legged and holding a sceptre, with the same figure in a manuscript of c. 1310–25 (Saint-Omer, Tournai or Ghent) in the John Rylands University Library in Manchester (figs. 13–14), it is tempting to imagine that he may be King Arthur, even though no capture of wild men is recounted in any of the Arthurian legends.[26] If this were the case, it could be that the standing knight at the front, wearing a helmet and holding an upright sword, who appears to

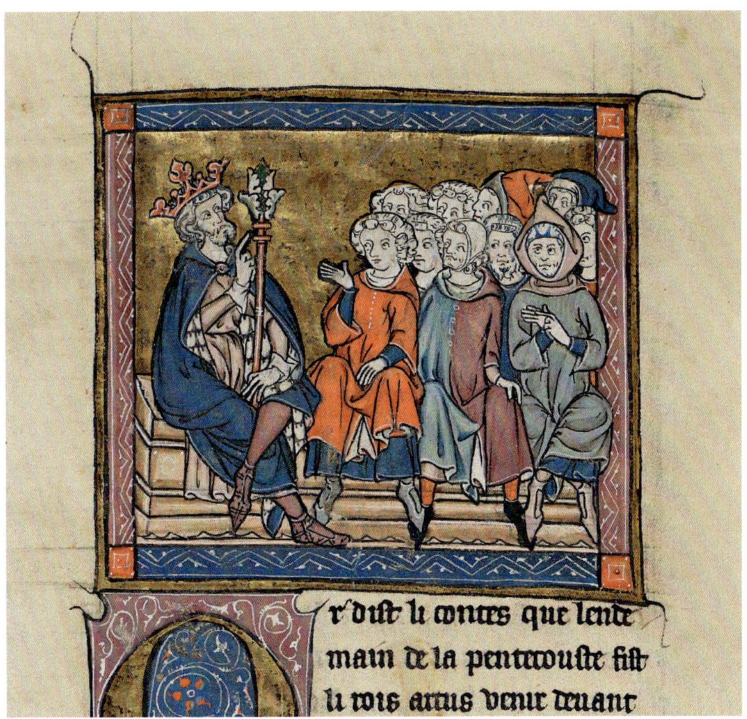

14. The knights of the round table tell of their
adventures to King Arthur, Lancelot-Grail
manuscript, Artois or Flanders (Saint-Omer,
Tournai or Ghent), c. 1310–25 (The John Rylands
University Library, Manchester, MS French 1, f. 114v)

be more interested in the queen on the battlements of the castle than the king, should be taken for the adulterous Lancelot, gazing towards the object of his love, Guinevere. Against this reading, just such a figure of a seated king represents both Alexander and Solomon on the Cracow, New York, Birmingham and Paris composite caskets (figs. 3, 8, 4, 10), seemingly following the same model, and Élisabeth Antoine has pointed out with circumspection that this should be viewed simply as the 'traditional pose of one in power'.[27]

Scenes of wild men on Gothic ivory caskets are very rare. Only two other caskets, one of them now lost and the other dismantled and incomplete, can be compared. The first, known as the 'Coffret de l'Académie', was in the collection of Claude Gros de Boze (d. 1753) in Paris, and already by that time broken up into pieces; only the whereabouts of the back panel is now known, in the Cloisters Collection of the Metropolitan Museum of Art in New York, but that shows a stag hunt.[28] Engravings of the casket were made in the eighteenth century, and reveal that the front panel was given over to scenes combining those of the lid and back of the Baird casket, although treating them in a different manner (fig. 15): wild men seize maidens; they are defeated in combat

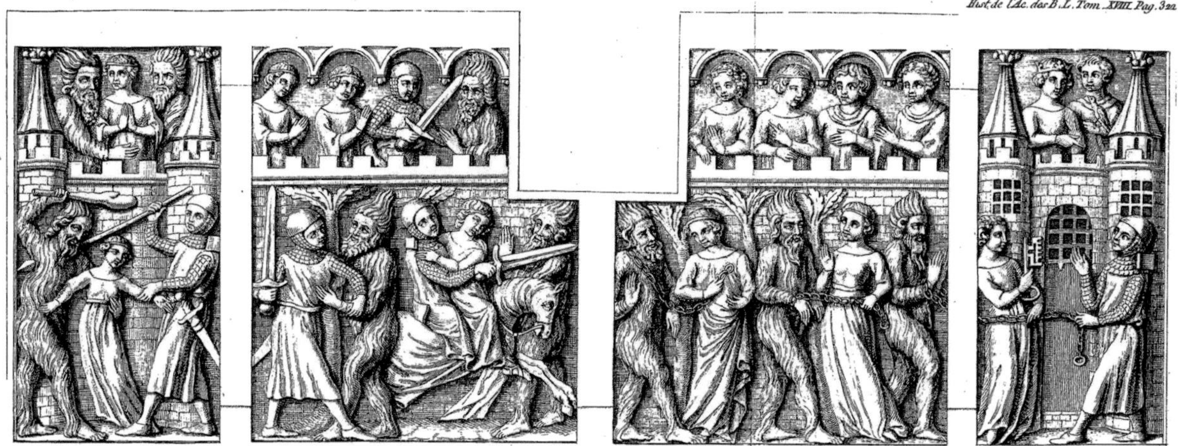

15. The front panel of the Académie casket,
shown in an engraving of 1753

by knights, who rescue the damsels; and the captive wild men, bound with chains, are then paraded by the maidens before the castle. The lid of the Académie casket, like the more standardized composite caskets, shows a tournament with jousting knights.

The second casket, like the Académie casket broken up into its constituent panels (its lid is now missing), is in the Musée du Louvre in Paris.[29] It is also the case that only the front panel is devoted to wild men, and here the narrative is much reduced (fig. 16). Only one maiden is abducted by a pair of wild men, who are then confronted by a single knight who stabs the first wild man with his lance and rescues the young lady; the wild men's lion crouches under the lock plate. On the right, two scenes show the aftermath of the knight's rescue, as he carries the maiden to safety on his charger and then delivers her before the castle's walls.

The lid of the Louvre casket is lost, but Danielle Gaborit-Chopin thought with good reason that – like the Académie casket – it must have shown a tournament scene.[30] It therefore seems that only the Baird casket devoted such an extensive space to the wild men, more than twice as much as other examples – although one must add the caveat that probably only a fraction of the original production of such caskets remains.

Images of wild men became increasingly common in the Gothic period, and by the fourteenth century they were seen across the artistic spectrum, in a wide range of media including ivory carvings, sculpture, enamels and goldsmiths' works, stained and painted glass, textiles and manuscript illumination.[31] In the context of such objects as the Baird casket and the ivory mirror case in the Wyvern Collection (fig. 17), wild men represented the

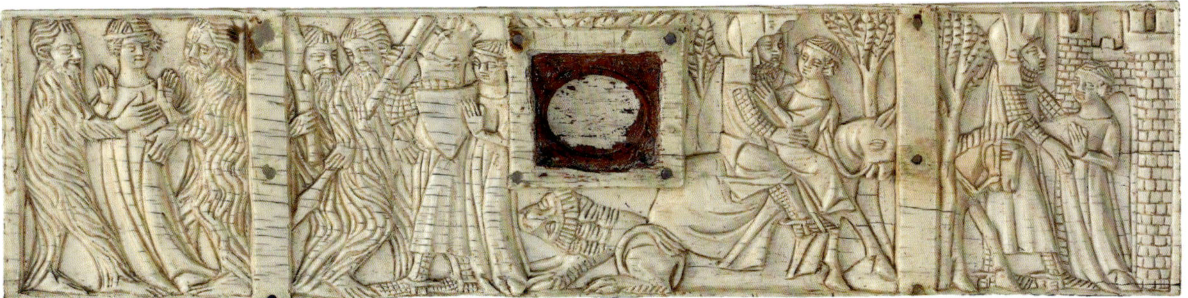

16. Front panel of a dismantled composite
casket, with the abduction of a maiden by
wild men and her rescue by a knight, French,
c. 1340 (Musée du Louvre, Paris)

untamed nature of human passion, and they could only be controlled by vir-
tuous knights who followed a civilized moral code, grounded in the tenets of
a Christian philosophy.[32] Notwithstanding the growing popularity of the wild
men, it is nevertheless unique – in the present state of knowledge – to find an
object which foregrounds their presence so conspicuously as the Baird casket.

The scenes on the lid and back of the casket are complemented by those on
the sides and front. On the left side two fully armoured knights on horseback
are engaged in combat with swords (plate 5), a scene replicated on several other
ivories, usually in the context of a tournament, where they vie for the attention of the watching ladies (fig. 18). As such, this display of knightly prowess is
not necessarily part of a larger story, nor do the knights have to be identified
as particular heroes of Arthurian legend, just as the jousting knights before
the Castle of Love on the lids of the *coffrets composites* are generic rather than
specific figures. Conversely, there is, of course, no shortage of plausible can-
didates if one were to speculate on their identity.[33]

The narrative becomes more complicated, however, when we turn to the
front of the casket (plate 6). The first scene, on the far left, shows a mounted
knight riding across a river, or through a lake, carrying a lady in his arms. He
appears to be the same figure as that shown on the Louvre casket, rescuing
the lady from the wild men: both knights have their visors raised, so better
to gaze into their maiden's eyes, and the lady places her left arm across the
knight's chest (figs. 19–20). The major difference is the addition of the water
(with fish) in the image on the Baird casket. It has been suggested, tentatively
and without conviction, that the scene is meant to show Tristan and Isolde,
when Tristan – disguised as a leper – carried Isolde across the Malpas river;
this is implausible, however, as a knight, not a beggar, is clearly depicted on
the casket, and other details of that story do not tally.[34] It might instead be
proposed that the knight could be Lancelot. Is the lady to be identified as

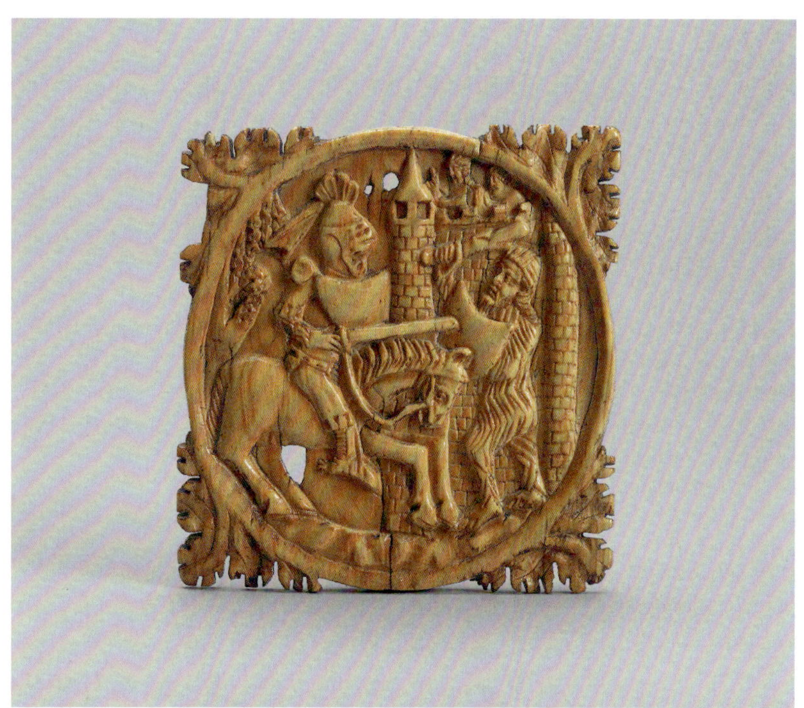

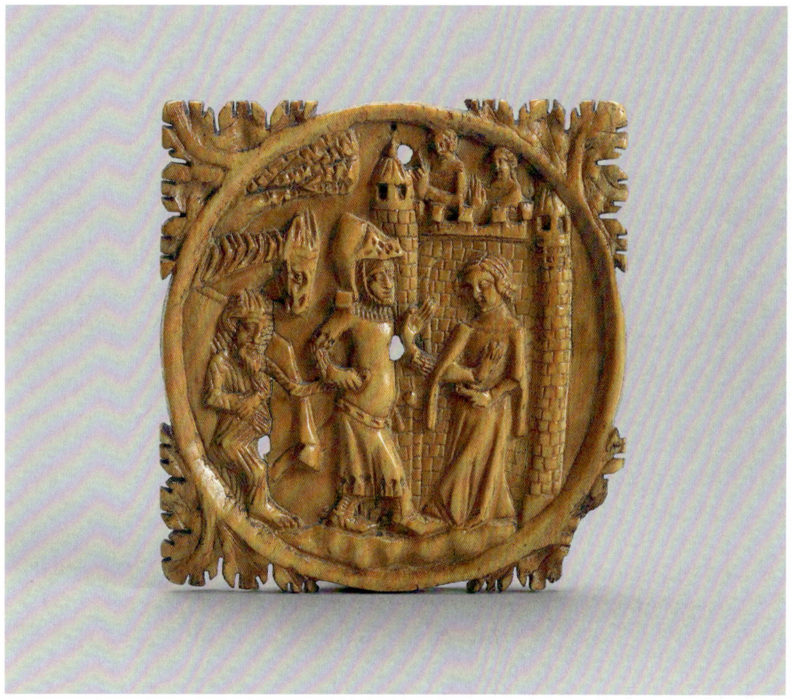

17. Mirror case with knight and wild man in combat, and the wild man's capture, French, c. 1340–50 (Wyvern Collection, London)

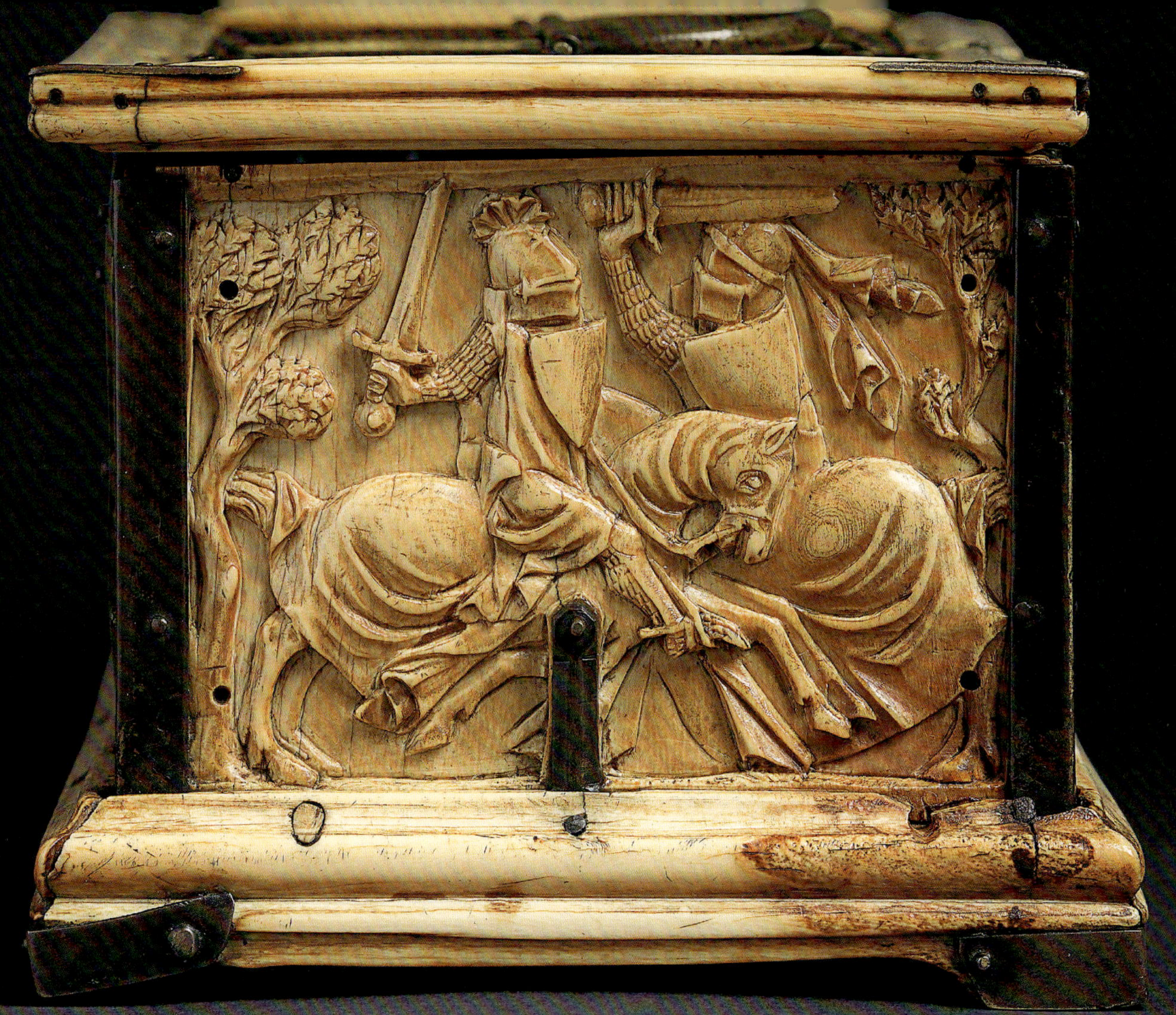

PLATE 5

The left side panel of the casket,
showing two mounted knights in combat

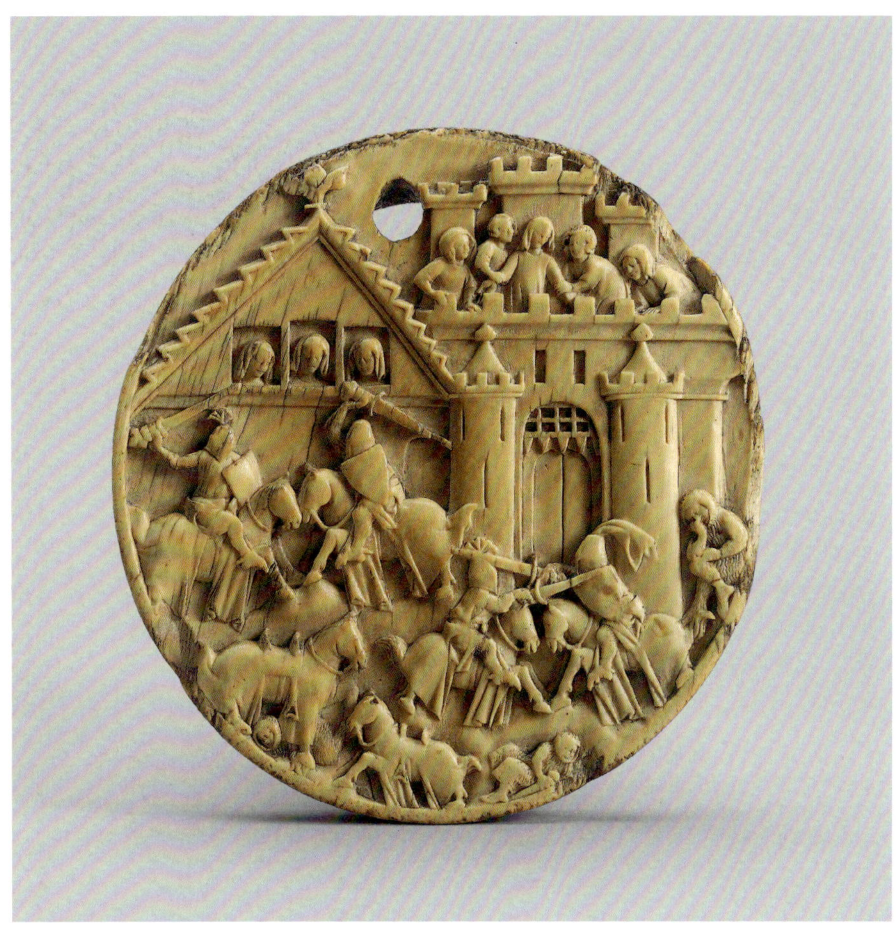

18. Mirror back with scenes from courtly
romance (Lancelot), French (Paris), c. 1300–10
(Wyvern Collection, London)

Guinevere, rescued from Meleagant, or is she simply the anonymous recipient of a chivalric good deed?[35]

The next scene shows an armoured knight with sword in hand, his visor
down and with the cloth plume of his helmet billowing behind, appearing to
ride at speed towards the castle in the adjoining image.[36] This impression of
speed, however, is contradicted by the presence of a squire or unarmoured
knight in front of him, who raises his right hand as if to engage in conversa-
tion and appears to hold the horse's rein.[37] Is it this same figure that is shown
kneeling in the next scene, to the right of the lock plate, and who appears to
be raising his right arm, indicating that his hand has been severed (fig. 21)?[38]
Had the knight with sword unsheathed cut off this unfortunate man's hand?
Above, on the battlements of the castle's gateway, the crowned king at the
right points to the injured figure and turns to speak to one of his knights,

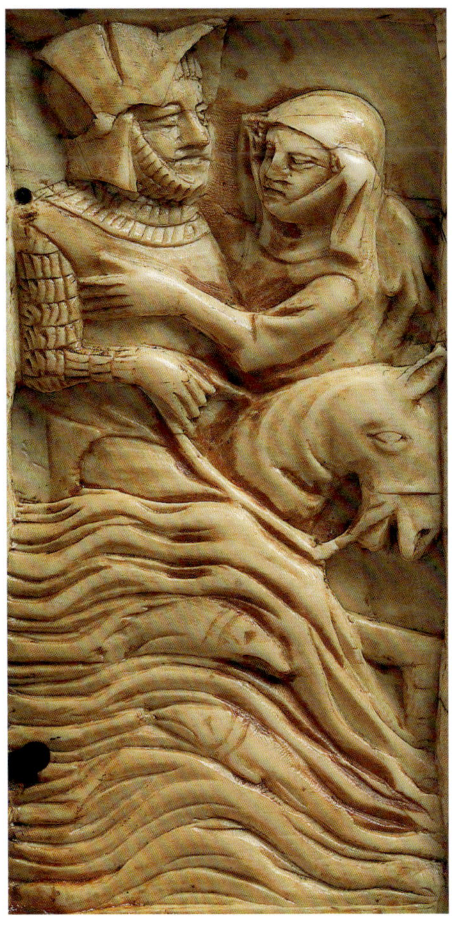

19. Detail of a mounted knight (Lancelot?) carrying a lady across the water, from the front of the Baird casket

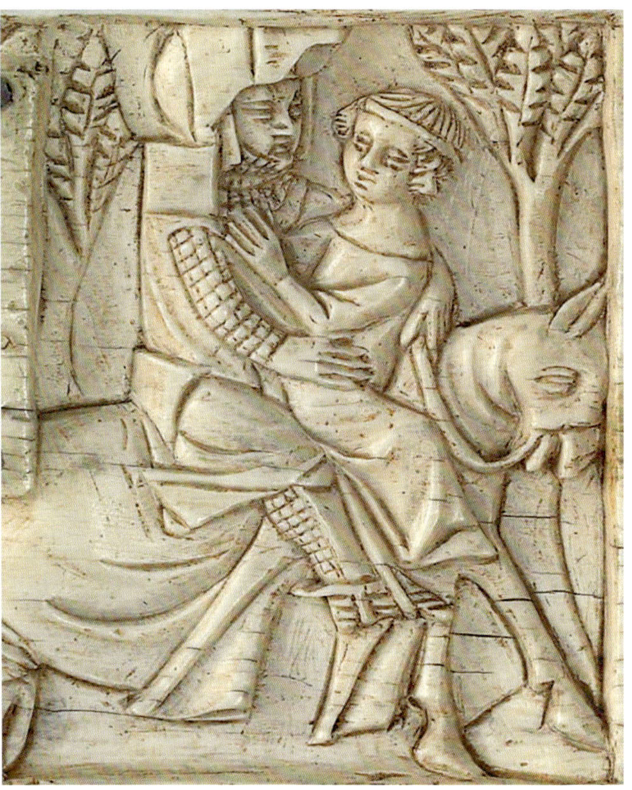

20. A mounted knight rescues a maiden, detail of the panel in fig. 16 (Musée du Louvre, Paris)

while on the left the queen appears to look towards the action in the previous scene, and her companion points in that direction. Again, this would make sense if the mounted knight were indeed Lancelot, given the relationship between him and Guinevere. Between the queen and the knight, at the centre of the group, a strange disembodied head stares out at the viewer.[39]

Paula Mae Carns and Elżbieta Musialik suggested that the kneeling figure with severed hand is meant to represent one of the knights who unsuccessfully attempted to pull the sword from the stone, and who was badly injured in the process.[40] That scene is not described in any of the written versions of the Grail Legend, however, nor is it shown in any other ivory carving or illuminated manuscript. This would indicate that instead it was probably an additional, different part of the Grail story, passed down orally and captured only by the carver of the casket, either at the request of the person

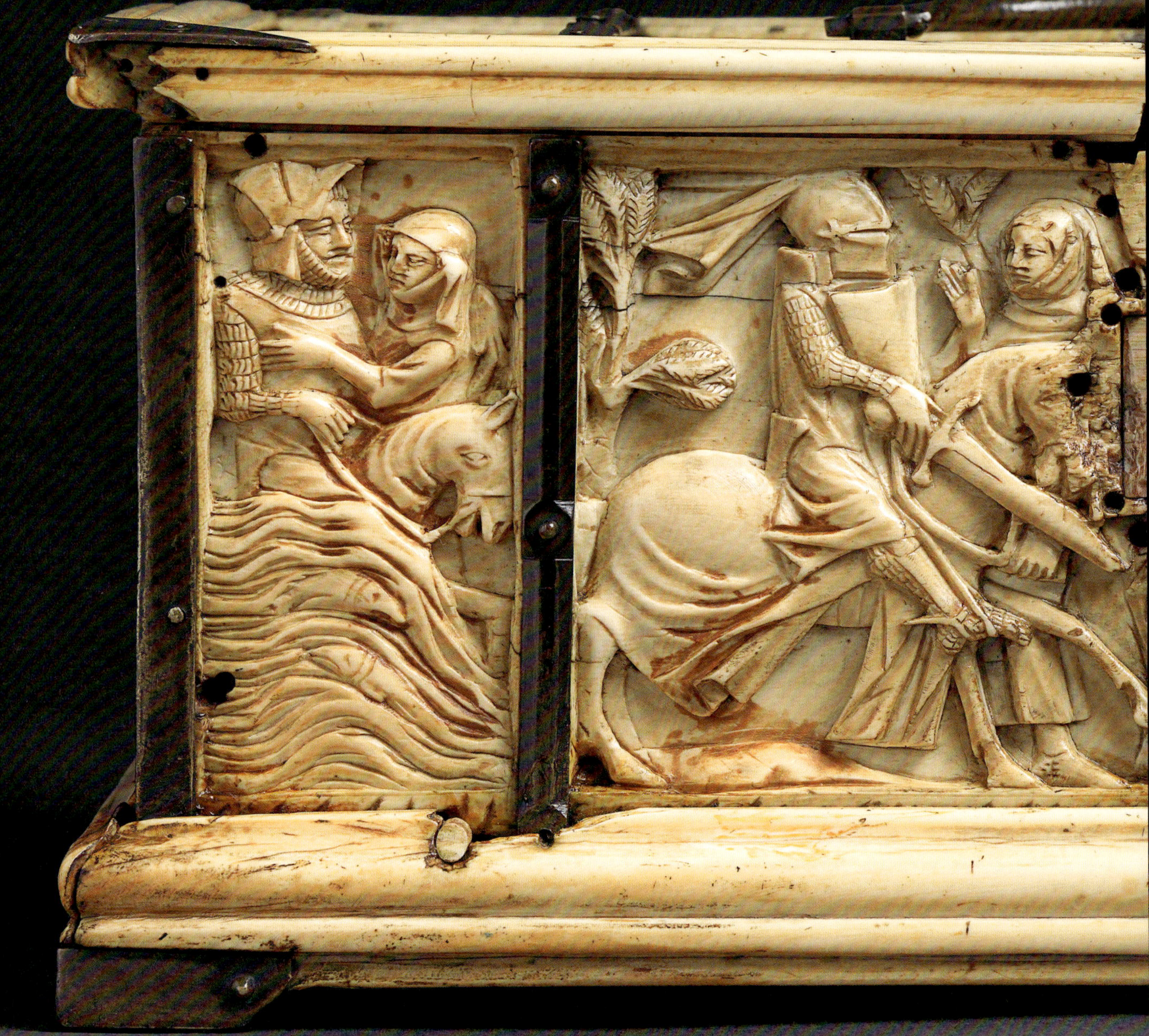

PLATE 6

The front of the casket, showing scenes of
Lancelot (?), a man with a severed hand,
and the sword above the Siege Perilous

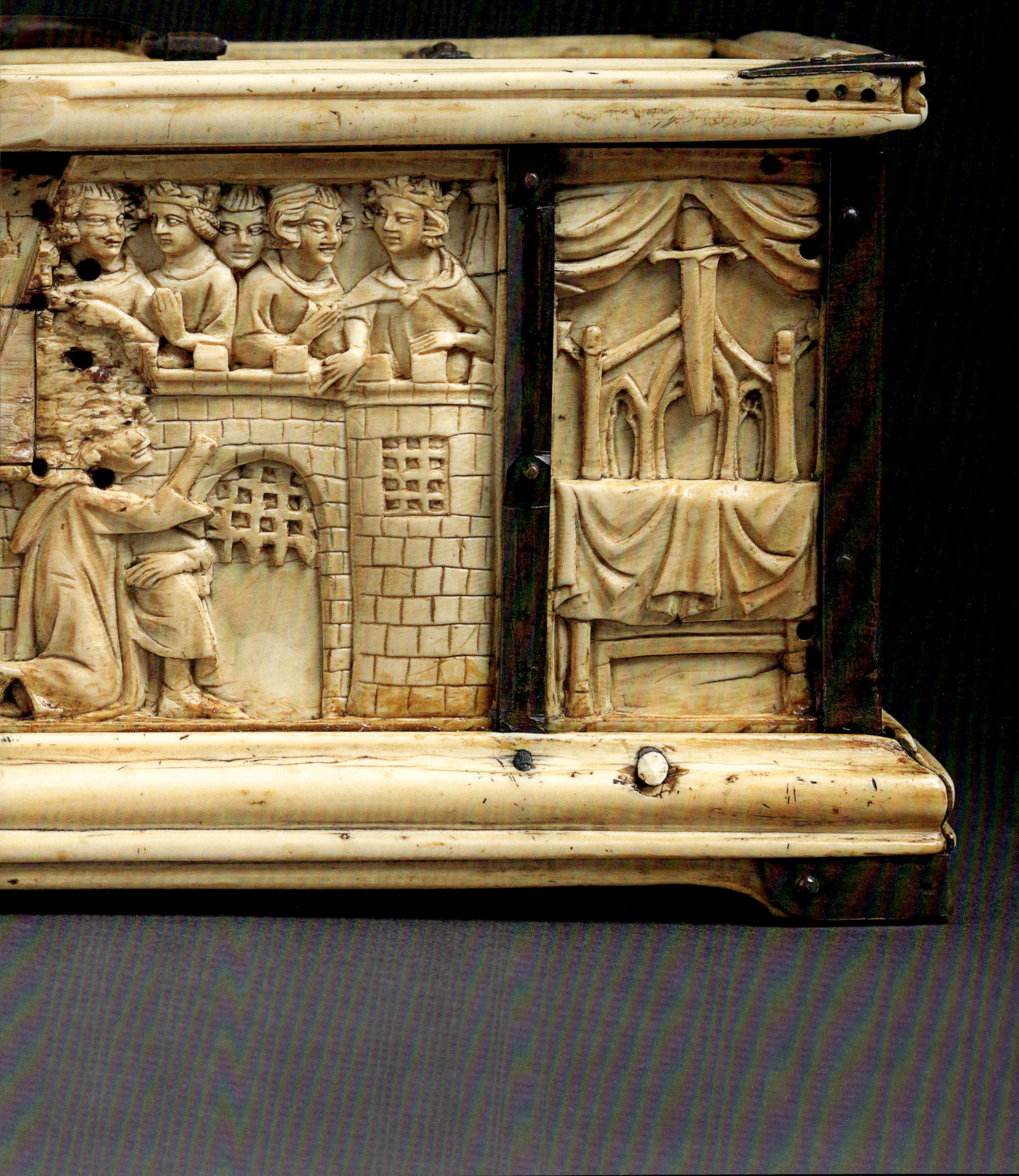

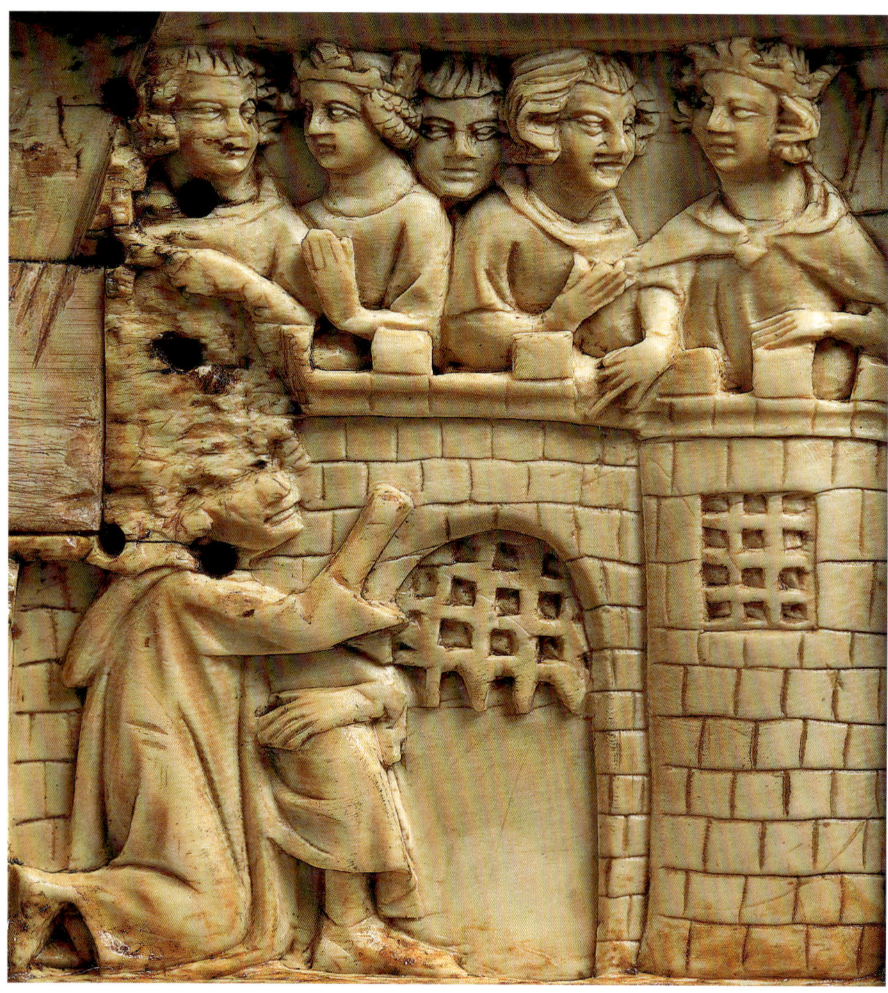

21. Detail of the man with the severed
hand on the front of the Baird casket

commissioning it or – less likely – at the whim of the workshop. It is also the
case that if these adjoining scenes at the centre of the front of the casket have
to do with Lancelot himself, there is again no known textual source for them.
Removing Lancelot from the reading entirely, one might more neutrally
interpret the actions of the knight on the back and front of the casket as those
of a loyal warrior devoted to both his king and queen.

Although there are actually three illustrations of various individuals losing
their hands in the fullest version of the Lancelot-Grail romance, kept in the
British Library in London (Add. 10292–4; 1315–20, Artois or Flanders), none
of these seems to match the image on the casket, nor to make sense in that
particular sequence.[41] The closest is the scene where the knight Sinarus, who
has had his right hand cut off, tells King Hargodabrans and King Gondefle

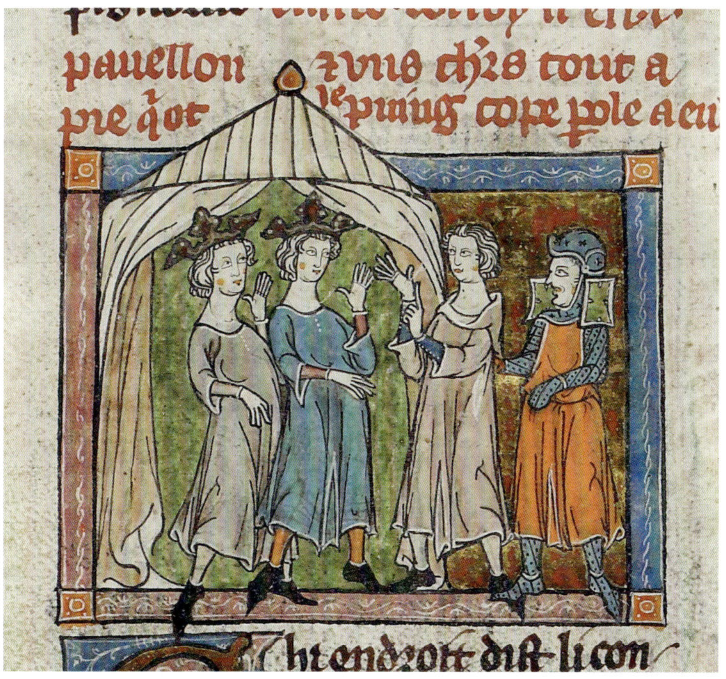

22. Sinarus, who has lost his right hand, stands before
King Hargodabrans and King Gondefle, Lancelot-
Grail manuscript, Artois or Flanders, 1315–20
(British Library, London, Add. 10292–4, f. 194v)

that their people are dead (fig. 22). But on the casket the crowned figure on
the left of the battlements is certainly a queen, and the previous and next
scenes bear no relation to the Sinarus episode, so it is likely that another –
more obscure – story is illustrated here. Could it be that the kneeling figure
is indeed the knight or squire shown standing before the mounted knight in
the previous scene? Was his right hand cut off by the knight for showing dis-
respect or for insulting the king or queen, or for theft, and that here he is
shown pleading with them for mercy and forgiveness?[42] Or had he doubted
the sanctity of the Grail, and been peremptorily punished? All these readings
would fit appropriately into the pictorial narrative, and would have been a
suitable illustration of the dispensing of justice or of quasi-divine retribution.

That the two central scenes on the front face of the casket were meant to be
read as sequential, as connected parts of the same story, might be supported
by comparison with contemporary manuscript illumination. Particularly germane in this connection is a *Lancelot propre* manuscript produced in Picardy
c. 1310–15, and now in the Morgan Library and Museum in New York (Ms. M.
805).[43] This manuscript is characterized by the extremely accomplished mini-
atures that spread across the three columns of the text, and which are all

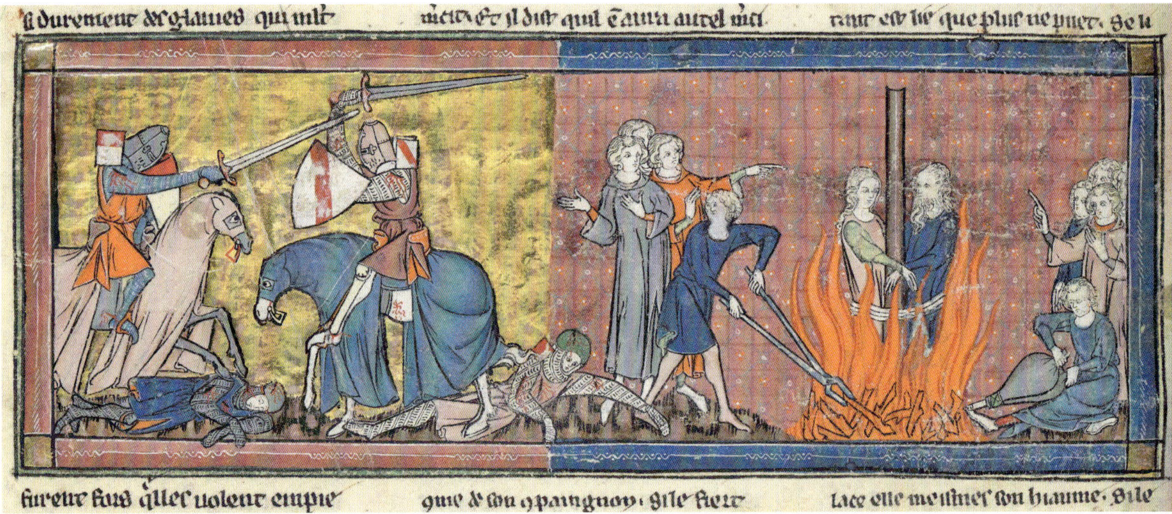

23. Lancelot and the False Guinevere, *Lancelot
propre* manuscript, Picardy, c. 1310–15
(The Morgan Library and Museum, New York,
MS. M. 805, f. 119v)

divided into separate halves. A typical example shows the story of the false
Guinevere, who is burnt at the stake with the knight Bertelay after plotting
to usurp the queen (on the right), following Lancelot's intervention (on the
left) (fig. 23). As Elizabeth Morrison has pointed out, the artist of the Lancelot
and false Guinevere miniature has linked the two halves by allowing one of
the dead knights to slump from the left scene into the right and by showing
the man arranging the pyre as looking back across the division to the battle
with Lancelot;[44] additionally, one of the three figures in the crowd gestures
towards Lancelot. In Morrison's words, 'these subtle visual touches serve to
emphasize the close relationship between the two halves and reinforce in the
viewer a sense of the immediate consequences of Lancelot's feat'. Just such a
connectivity can be detected in the two scenes of the Baird casket, where the
queen looks back towards the knight, and her companion's gesture – pointing
towards the previous scene – binds the two images together (fig. 24). If the
proposed reading of the scenes on the front of the Baird casket is accepted,
they show – as does the Morgan illumination – the ruthless consequences of
traitorous or wicked actions.

From a stylistic point of view, it is of interest that the riding knight on
the Baird casket – and that on the left short side – seems to be based on the
same model, with minor variations, as that seen on the casket in the Barber
Institute in Birmingham and some of the other composite caskets (figs. 24,
25). Although the knight of the Baird casket holds a sword rather than a lance,
the fall of the drapery of the horse's caparison is very similar, and it is as if the

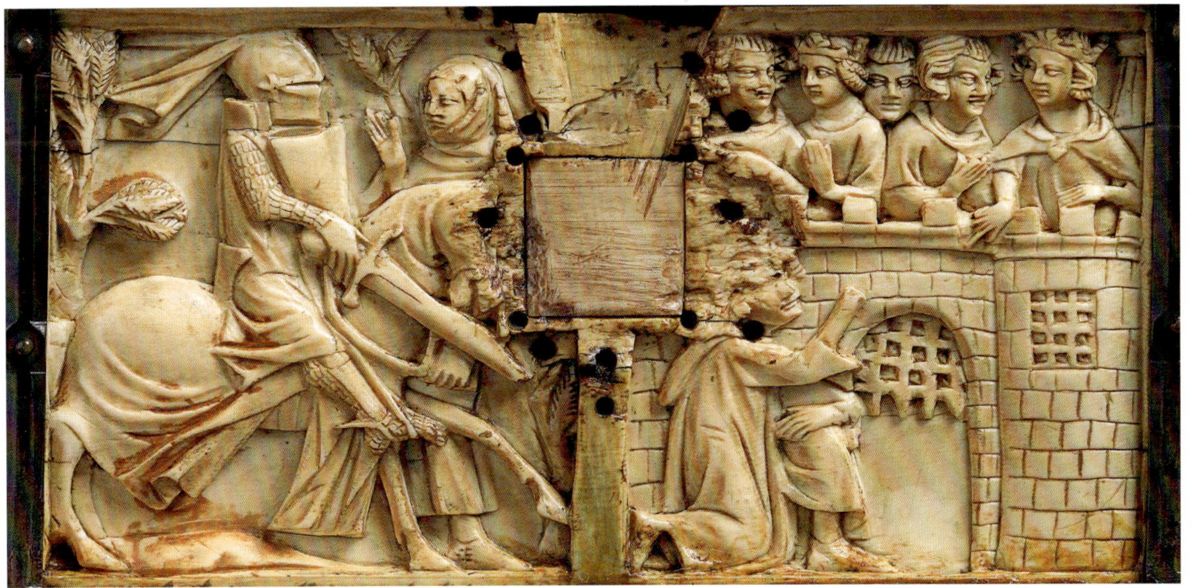

24. Detail of the two central scenes
on the front of the Baird casket

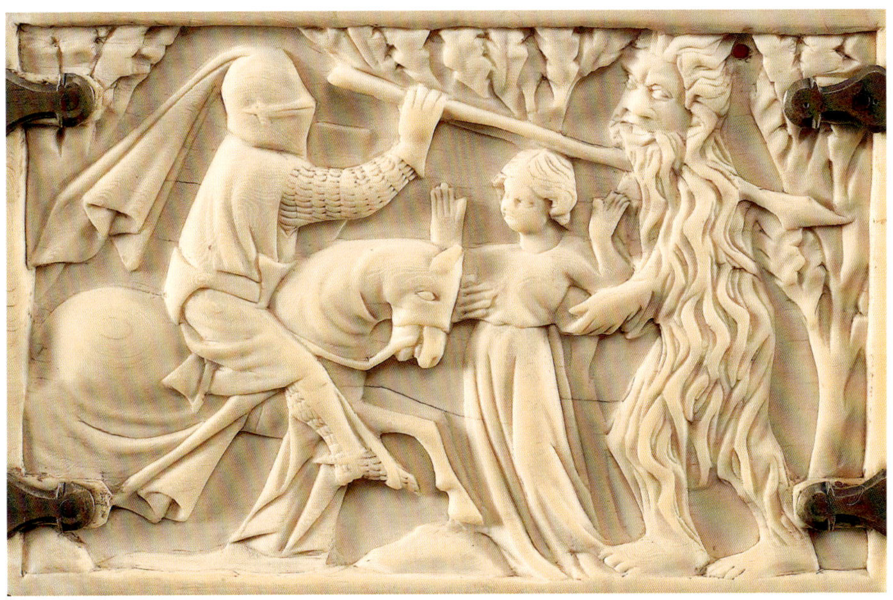

25. A knight rescues a maiden from a wild man,
right side of the composite casket in fig. 4
(Barber Institute of Fine Arts, Birmingham)

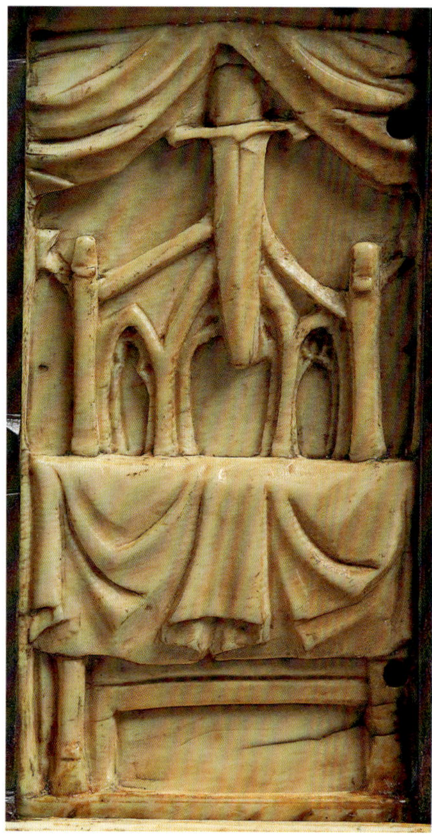

26. Detail of the sword above the Siege
Perilous on the front of the Baird casket

figure of the standing man has replaced the abducted young maiden of the
Barber casket. This, together with other compositional quotes elsewhere on
the Baird casket, suggests either an exposure on the part of the carver to one
or more of the composite caskets or his knowledge of a common model book.

The last image on the front of the casket, at the far right, is seemingly more
straightforward than the other scenes on the same side. It appears to show
the sword that only Galahad – Lancelot's son – could free from the stone,
floating above the vacant Siege Perilous of the Round Table in Camelot,
which Galahad was then entitled to occupy (fig. 26).[45] Lancelot, on account of
his adulterous desire for Guinevere, was considered less deserving. A similar
image of the Siege, at the centre of the Round Table and with a cloth canopy
above, is found in a slightly later Italian manuscript illumination showing
Galahad arriving to take up his place (fig. 27).

The right and final side of the casket shows an angel genuflecting and
holding the chalice-like Grail before an assembly of knights (plate 7). The
twelve knights of the Round Table, their shields hung behind them, join their

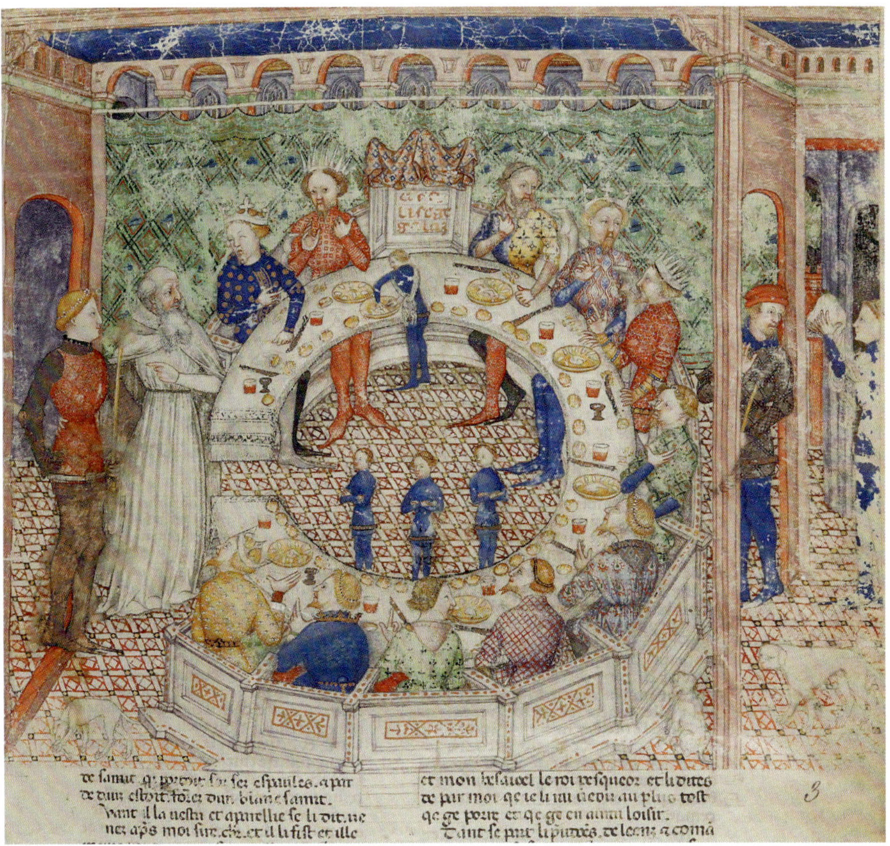

27. Galahad comes to the Siege Perilous, *Lancelot du Lac* manuscript, North Italian (Lombardy), c. 1380–85 (Bibliothèque nationale de France, Paris, Fr. 343, f. 3)

hands in prayer, while the central figure of Galahad, the Christ-like chosen one, holds the upright sword shown in the previous scene, signifying his pre-eminence as the greatest knight; the parted curtains above him represent the cloth canopy of the Siege Perilous on which he sits. The Round Table is here shown as a straight, bench-like table, referencing the Last Supper of Christ and the Apostles, and other images of similar scenes, both contemporary and later, must have intentionally brought to mind the relation between the Grail vision and the New Testament (figs. 28–29).[46] But there are adjustments – or perhaps a wilful conflation – at play here, and in no other representations of Galahad at the Round Table is he shown holding a sword. This must be significant, and may indicate the type of recipient for whom the casket was intended.

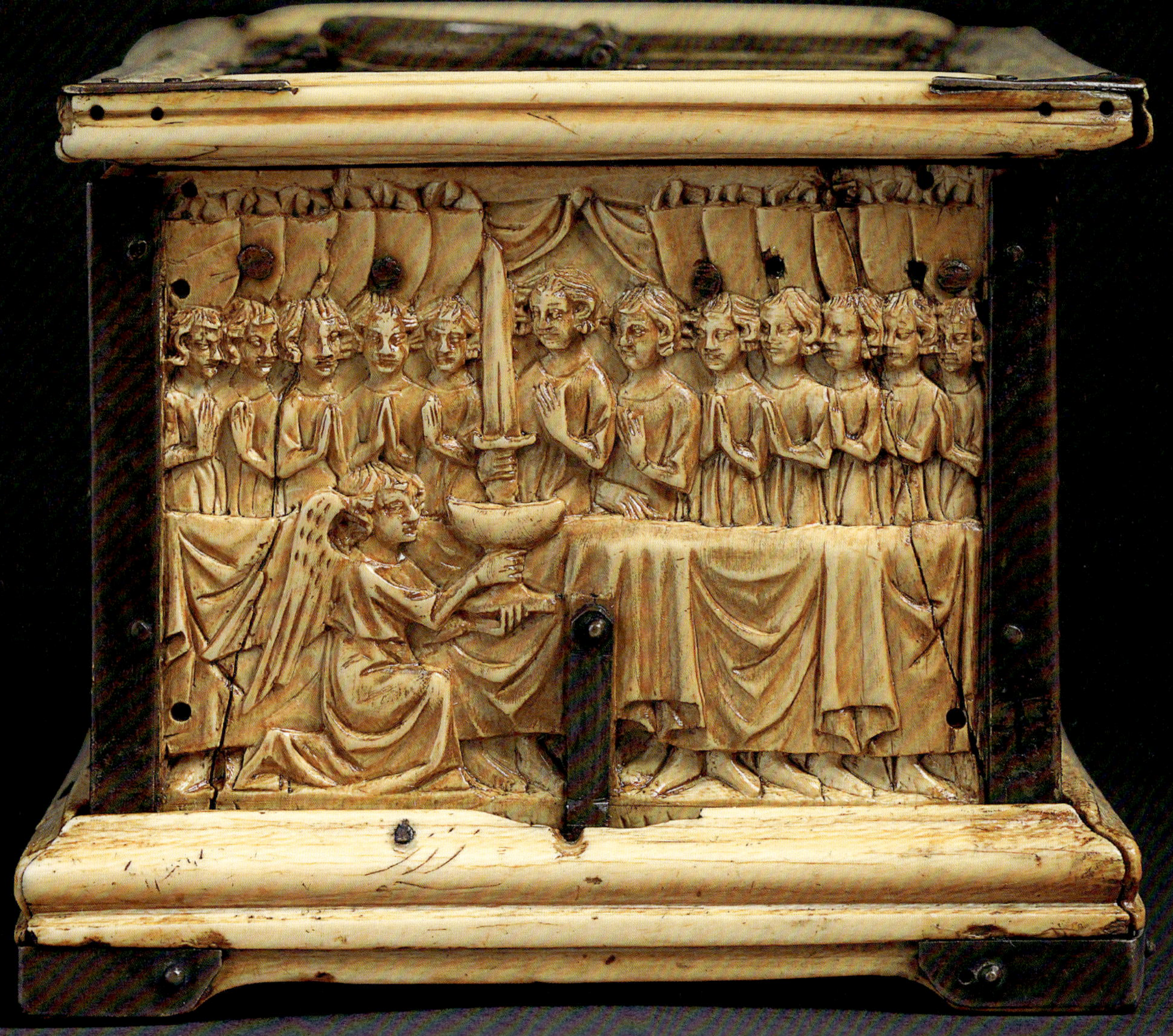

PLATE 7
The right side panel of the casket,
showing the Vision of the Grail

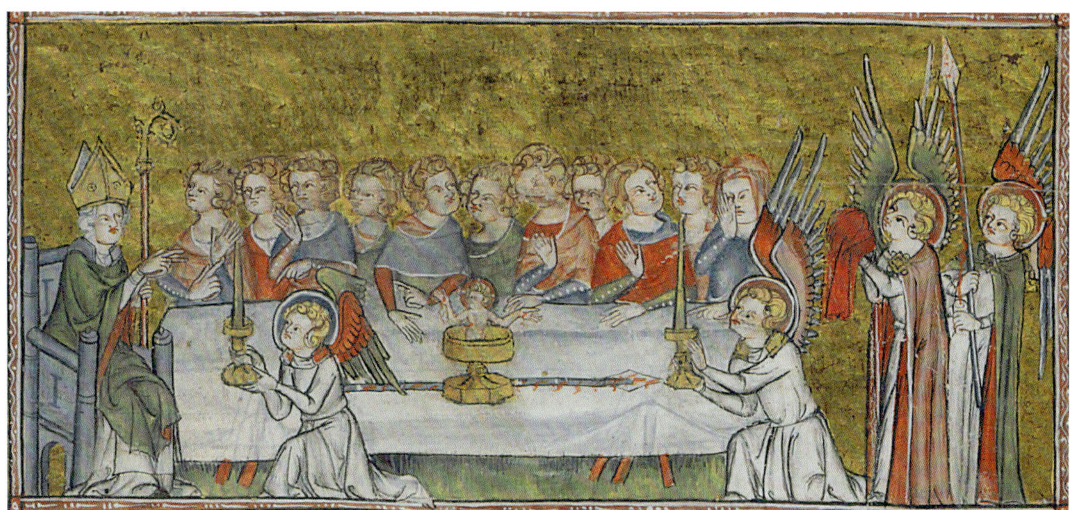

28. The Mass of the Holy Grail, *La Queste del Saint-Graal* manuscript, French (Paris), 1351 (Bibliothèque nationale de France – Bibliothèque de l'Arsenal, Ms. 5218, f. 88r)

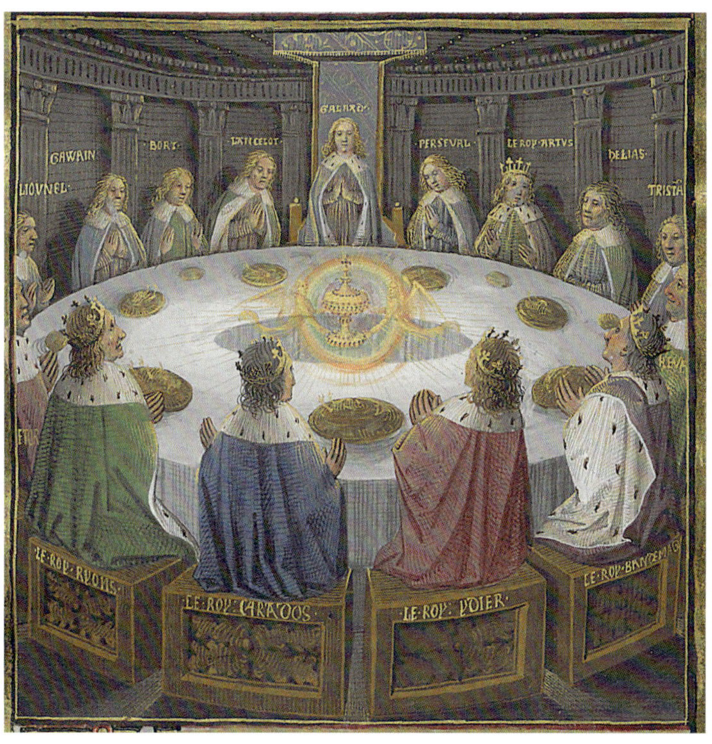

29. The Holy Grail appears at the Round Table, *La Queste del Saint-Graal* manuscript, French, 1475 (Bibliothèque nationale de France, Paris, Fr. 116, f. 610v)

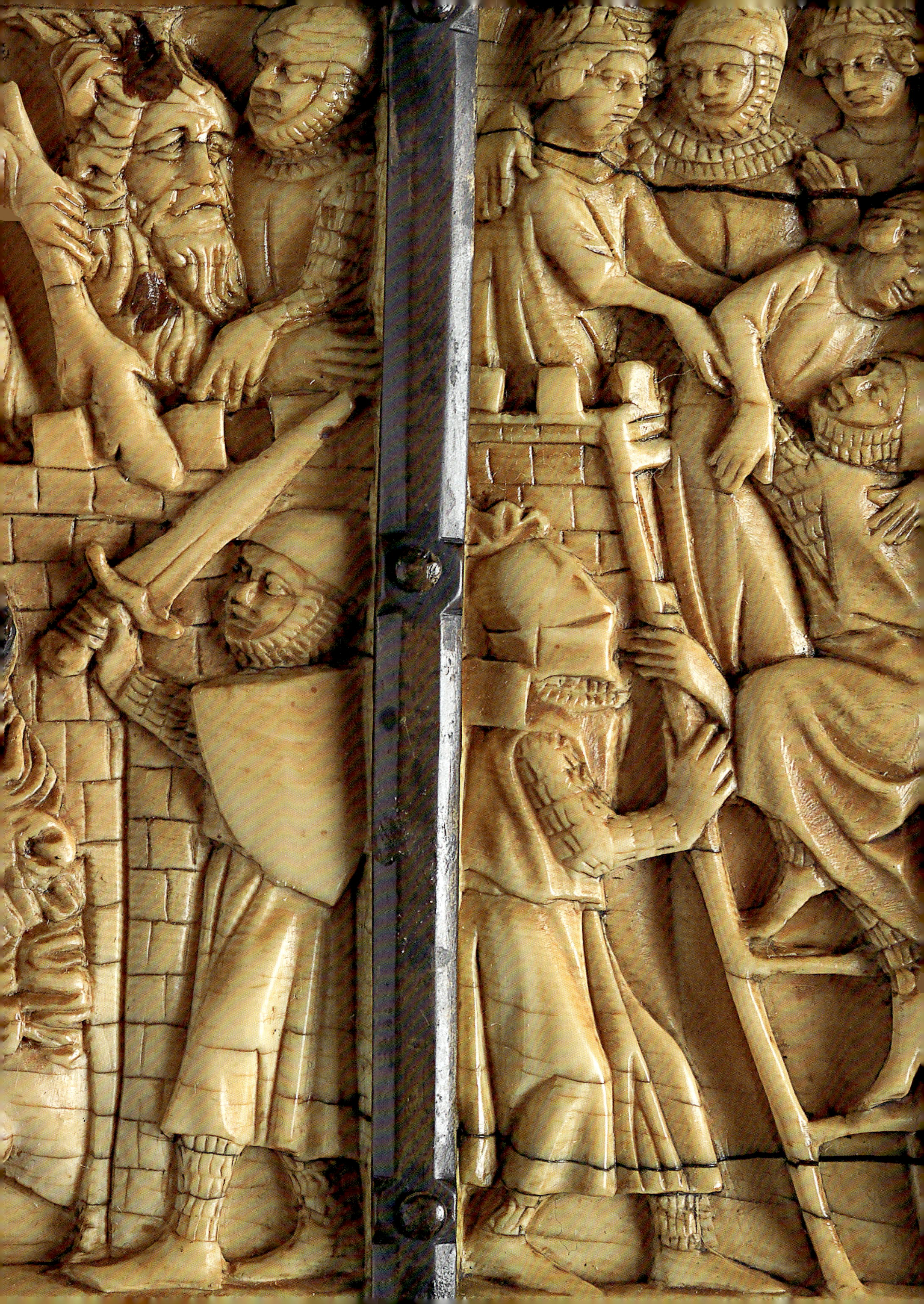

The Date and Place of Production of the Casket, and its Recipient

Given the compositional and stylistic connections that the Baird casket has with the caskets of the *coffrets composites* group, some of which have been pointed out in the previous pages, there can hardly be a significant difference in the date of production. The dates given to these caskets – in the last thirty years of scholarship – have ranged over the first half of the fourteenth century, with a tendency most recently to place them in the years 1300–30.[47] Élisabeth Antoine-König has proposed that the armour seen on the caskets, showing helms with visors, poleyns (knee protection), greaves (protectors placed over mail chausses to shield the front of the tibia), ailettes (round or square shoulder protectors) and the absence of arm protection, indicates a date of 1300–20, and certainly no later than 1325.[48] All these features are seen on the Baird casket (plates 5, 6).

Notwithstanding these observations, there can be no doubt that the armour type described by Antoine-König continued to be seen on ivories of the second quarter of the fourteenth century and even beyond, as is evident from its appearance on the front panel of the dismembered casket in the Musée du Louvre (fig. 16). This has plausibly been dated to c. 1340–50 by Danielle Gaborit-Chopin, who remarked that its style, although lively, is slightly summary and rapidly executed, and very different from the carvings of the first decades of the century.[49] The same applies to the related ivory mirror case with the knight and the wild man in the Wyvern Collection, although here the knight wears a reinforced breastplate, clearly indicating its slightly later date (fig. 17). Additionally, a French plaque from a set of writing tablets, in the Victoria and Albert Museum, certainly to be dated c. 1360–80, shows a knight dressed in the same armour as the earlier fourteenth-century examples.[50]

The Baird casket appears to occupy a stylistic territory between the finest examples of the composite casket group and the Louvre casket and Wyvern mirror case, and a date in the region of 1320–30 would therefore seem most appropriate. Where it was made is perhaps more of an enigma. Paris would be the obvious assumption, because of the universally accepted place of production for the composite caskets and the overwhelming amount of documentary evidence linked to patronage and supply in the French capital, and this may be correct. But other artistic centres where ivory was carved in the fourteenth and fifteenth centuries have also been identified, including England, Germany (Cologne and Lorraine), Italy (Venice and elsewhere), Flanders (Bruges), Spain and even Norway.[51] Could the Baird casket have come from a non-Parisian atelier, especially as the stylistic difference of the carvings from some of these workshops appears to be negligible?

As has been mentioned above, the choice of scenes on the casket sets it apart from the core group of the other composite caskets. Indeed, some of the images – not seen in any other carvings and not readily intelligible to the modern viewer – suggest that the person for whom it was made (or the patron who commissioned it for giving, assuming it was not produced simply for general sale) was involved in their choice. Unlike the composite caskets, which celebrate love and the relations between men and women, the scenes on the Baird casket are given over to the gallantry of knights, to chivalry, combat and to the sanctity of the Grail. They highlight the triumph of civilized mores and a constant quest for the sacred, so that these scenes, 'in which the wild man is a kidnapper and the knight a saviour ... have a moralizing tone and should be treated as the *exemplum*'.[52] This overarching male emphasis therefore seems to indicate that this particular casket was intended for the use of a knight rather than a woman, and the emphasis throughout on the power of the sword reinforces this reading. All the knights shown on the casket wield a sword, not once employing a lance, and this weapon conspicuously appears on the lid and all four sides of the box, culminating in its appearance at Camelot, in front of the Siege Perilous and held by Galahad, directly above the Grail, at the round table. The sword is the dominant actor here, and links all the scenes on the casket.

Another ivory casket of about the same date, dedicated to scenes from the early life of Perceval and with a lid showing four saints, must also – because of its subject matter – have been intended as a gift to a knight (fig. 30). As plausibly proposed by Martine Meuwese, the recipient was perhaps a young man, like Perceval, and the casket would undoubtedly have been a very appropriate present 'on the occasion of his entrance into the knighthood'.[53]

If made for a knight, as must be overwhelmingly likely, the Baird casket may have been meant to contain letters or documents, perhaps a seal matrix or badges, but probably not jewellery. As has been argued elsewhere, the small locks on these ivory boxes – rather tellingly torn off in the case of the Baird casket – must have acted simply as a barrier to opportunistic opening; the inherent fragility of the caskets, without a wooden or metal core, would not have deterred a serious thief looking for valuables.[54]

By the beginning of the fourteenth century, the Arthurian romances were widely popular, spread through the writings of Chrétien de Troyes and followers, and the literary accounts were translated into visual form across different media, but particularly in illuminated manuscripts.[55] It is of interest that some of the most complete and richly illustrated versions of the Lancelot-Grail (including the *Estoire, Merlin, Lancelot, Queste* and *Morte Artu*), were produced in the regions of Picardy, Artois and Flanders, at centres such as Saint-Omer, Thérouanne, Tournai and Ghent, in the years 1310–25, and there was clearly a thriving market for them: figs. 14, 22 and 23 are examples of the

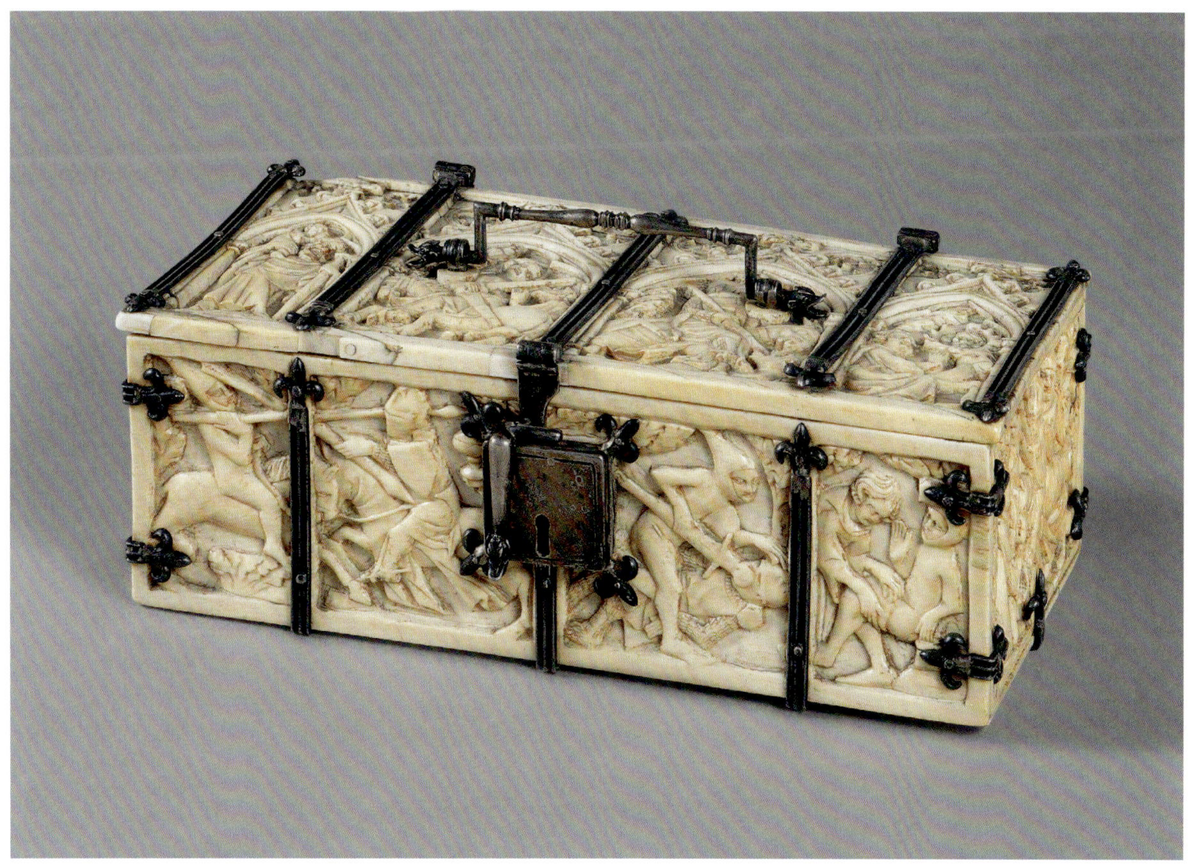

30. Casket with scenes from the story of Perceval,
with four saints on the lid, French (Paris),
c. 1310–30 (Musée du Louvre, Paris)

work of two of these manuscript illuminators.[56] May the singular choice of
scenes on the Baird casket, so different from those on the Parisian composite
caskets, indicate an origin in this region? Or was the idiosyncratic narrative
instead simply due to the particular instructions of a specific patron in Paris?

As we have seen, the casket appears to have been in the South Netherlands,
probably Flanders, by the middle of the fifteenth century, when it was
repaired, its base added and the lid extended at the edges. It may also be significant that Andrew Baird went to Flanders with his nephew Thomas Baird
in 1615, so it could have been acquired there on that occasion.[57] This is no
more than a hypothesis, however, and even if it were established as true it
would not prove that the casket was made in Flanders. Parisian Gothic ivories
were widely exported, and there is, unfortunately, no corpus of demonstrably
Flemish ivory carvings to which the casket could be compared. Moreover, we
have seen that some of the figures on the Baird casket show a clear knowledge

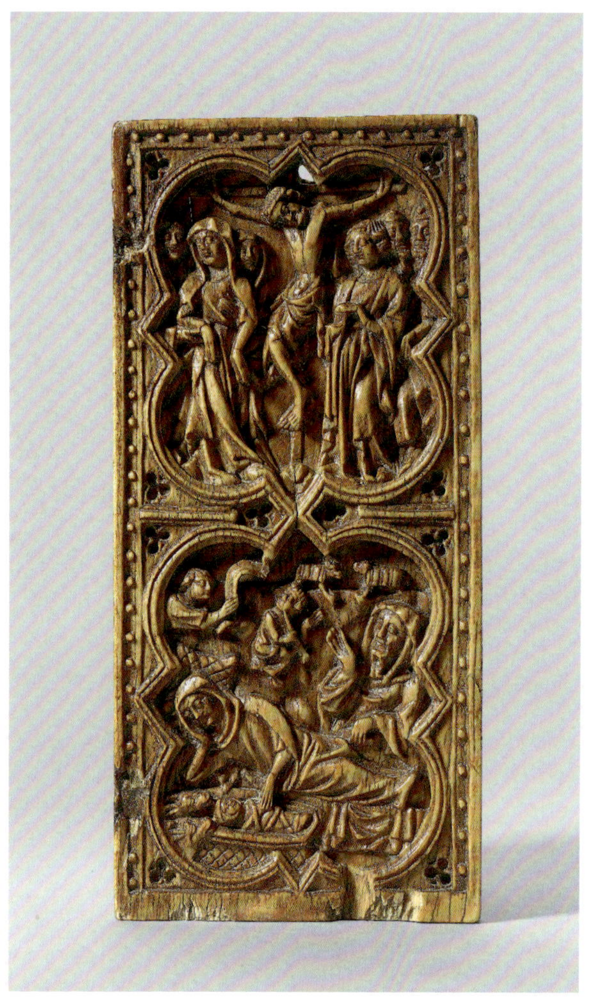

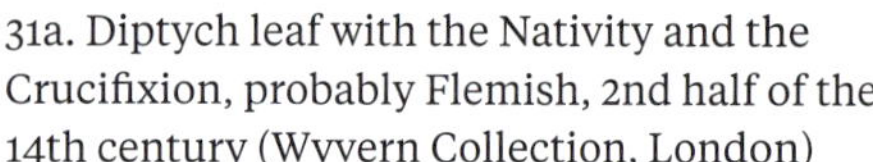

31a. Diptych leaf with the Nativity and the Crucifixion, probably Flemish, 2nd half of the 14th century (Wyvern Collection, London)

31b. Back of diptych leaf in fig. 31b, showing inscription

of those on Parisian ivories, although this in itself does not prove an origin in Paris. Suffice it to say, however, that non-Parisian versions of the composite caskets do appear to have been made, as evidenced by a detached lid in Boulogne and possibly by the 'Lord Gort' casket, now in Winnipeg.[58]

Wherever the casket was produced, it must have continued to be valued and appreciated long after its date of manufacture in the first half of the fourteenth century. The fact that it was repaired and expanded in Flanders over a century later raises several interesting questions. Who owned it by the middle of the fifteenth century, and had it been passed down within the family of its first owner, so that it had become a dynastic heirloom? Why was there a reverence for such an object when there appears to have been a thriving industry in Flanders producing ivory and bone caskets that obviously fulfilled the same purpose? Why repair the old when the new might have provided a more up-to-date product in better condition?

A notable parallel to the casket is provided by another ivory carving kept in the Wyvern Collection. This is the diptych leaf showing the Nativity and the Crucifixion which, together with its pair now in the Museum of Art of the Rhode Island School of Design showing the Annunciation and the Adoration of the Magi, appears to be a product of a Flemish workshop of the second half of the fourteenth century (figs. 31a–b).[59] Like the Baird casket, the diptych must have been treasured despite, or perhaps because of, being over a hundred years old: in this case, the proof is provided by the inscription carved on the back of the leaves, which reads in translation 'Donaes de Moer gave this to my young lady Adriane de Vos in the year 1478'.[60] This is particularly significant, not just for the diptych but also for the casket, as it demonstrates clearly the former's continued use in the 1470s, and also because it shows that such things were still valued by those in the highest tier of society. Donaes de Moer (d. 1483) was one of the most distinguished merchants of Bruges, and together with his young wife Adriane (d. 1509) he commissioned several important art works in the city.[61] We do not know whether Donaes de Moer bought the antique diptych or whether it had been owned by his family (probably more likely), but the fact that it was deemed worthy as a gift – alongside the many prestigious works of art he ordered – is extremely meaningful.

It is likely that the casket was equally valued by its mid-fifteenth-century owner, being sufficiently prized to ensure that it would be repaired and embellished. Its subject matter must have held as strong an attraction to this later owner as it did to its original possessor, and it is worthy of note that the Flemish fifteenth-century casket workshops do not appear to have produced boxes with scenes of romance.[62] Most of their caskets were concerned with religious iconography or – if secular – were made up of individual panels of dancers, animals, jousting, the hunt, and other figures, including wild men; a casket of this type, therefore, would have held a certain cachet, especially if it was linked to a particular figure or had a strong family connection. Whether a product of a Parisian workshop or a regional variation, the Baird casket has retained the power to enthral and engross the modern viewer.

APPENDIX
RADIOCARBON DATING
OF THE CASKET

Two samples of ivory were shaved from the rear of the front and right side panel of the casket for radiocarbon testing by RCD Lockinge, Wantage, Oxfordshire, in March 2025 (refs: RCD-10382 for the front panel, RCD-10383 for the right side panel). The calibration plots, showing the calendar age ranges, are reproduced here. It should of course be remembered that the Radiocarbon test gives an approximate date for the ivory (i.e. the death of the elephant), not for the carving; the comparatively imprecise date-range is no substitute for close art-historical dating, although the test frequently provides clarification when questions of authenticity may be raised. It should also be pointed out that the death of the elephant might have occurred at any point within the calibrated calendar age range, so a slightly later terminal date of the time bracket (as in the case of RCD-10383) does not provide a definitive terminus post quem for the carving (I am grateful to Jill Walker at RCD Lockinge for discussing the results with me).

For the first test, of the front panel (RCD-10382), a date of 1228–96 with a 95.4% degree of probability was obtained. The second test, of the right side panel (RCD-10383), gave a date of 1280-1394 with a 95.4% degree of probability, with a 46.9% degree of probability within that range for a date of 1280–1325. There is therefore nothing in the two results to preclude a date of c. 1320–30 for the casket, arrived at on the grounds of art-historical analysis.

It is of interest that the results might indicate that the panels were carved from ivory drawn from two different elephants, rather than being sourced from the same tusk. The other four plaques of the casket (including the base plate) have not been tested, and it may be that at least one of these would have yielded an identical result to one of the two panels that were subjected to scientific analysis. One is prompted here to think of the size of the workshop responsible for the Baird casket, and of its access to supplies of ivory, either ready-cut plaques or whole tusks.[63]

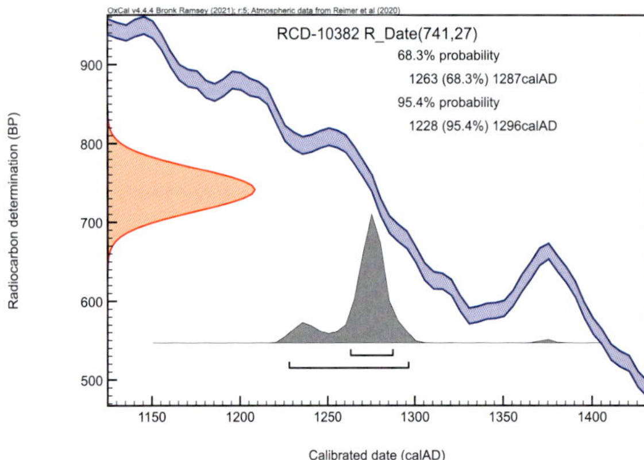

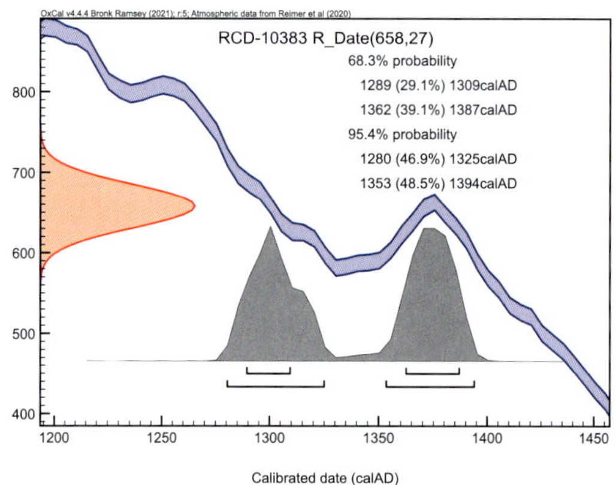

1 Williamson 2019, cat. no. 73, pp. 150–53.

2 *Five Centuries: Furniture, Paintings & Works of Art*, lot 493.

3 All references in the present publication are to the 1857 edition, a copy of which is kept in the National Library of Scotland (A.114.a.3.) in Edinburgh and is available in digital form.

4 The manuscript is Edinburgh, National Library of Scotland, Adv. MS. 32.6.12.

5 Fraser 1857, pp. 18–19. In a footnote on p. 19, Fraser states that 'This relique is in my possession', and the casket subsequently passed by descent through his family until its sale in 2021. Fraser was William Baird's great grandson (Bulloch 1934, p. 9).

6 The slip is now kept in the files of the Wyvern Research Institute.

7 Fraser 1857, pp. 45–46, letters X and XI.

8 Ibid., pp. 48–49, letter XIII (10 February 1615).

9 Ibid., p. 51, letter XVI.

10 Ibid., p. 65, 20 November 1632, letter from James Baird to George Baird.

11 Musialik 2022 and 2024.

12 There is a label on the inside of the lid, undoubtedly of late nineteenth- or early twentieth-century type, with the number '231' written in ink. This is probably an inventory number connected with the holdings at Tornaveen, perhaps referring to a probate or insurance listing.

13 Wyvern Collection inv. no. 3005.

14 See Koechlin 1911 for examples of ivories with a pre-nineteenth-century history, and, additionally, Koechlin 1924, p. 42.

15 The term '*coffrets composites*' was coined by Raymond Koechlin, who went on to discuss the group at length (Koechlin 1924, I, pp. 484–508, II, cat. nos. 1281–87).

16 Musialik 2022, p. 9, n. 4; McLaren Young 1947, p. 17; Williamson 2024, pp. 11–20, 27; Davies 2017, pp. 247–48, and for other caskets owned by Douce, see pp. 248–50.

17 The so-called 'Lord Gort' casket, now in Winnipeg, is excluded here as it differs in style and composition (see note 58).

18 There is no sign of a wooden base, mentioned in Musialik 2022 (p. 10).

19 Musialik (2022, p. 11) noted that 'the interior of the casket on one side is lined with cloth, which is probably a later addition'; this has now been removed. There are also a small number of incised symbols near the edges of the plaques, possibly made in connection with the assembly or repair of the casket.

20 Even if some of these mounts have been replaced, they certainly follow the original fittings.

21 The square hole for the lock plate has now been filled with a faux ivory panel, replacing the wood insert that was present at the time of the auction in 2021. A restoration of the casket was carried out in October 2023 by Rupert Harris Conservation Ltd, London, and a report is lodged with the Wyvern Collection.

22 Williamson 2019, cat. no. 146; see also cat. no. 148 for a different type, with flat lid, and another casket in the Victoria and Albert Museum (Williamson and Davies 2014, cat. no. 175).

23 The lower borders of the casket and both borders of the lid were cross-hatched at this time to aid the adhesion of the additions, and ivory pegs added further strength to the new base.

24 There are substantial traces of a brown residue on some of the reliefs, especially on the front panel, but no evidence of painted highlights.

25 A lion or lions are shown elsewhere (see fig. 16) as companions of wild men; see also Musialik 2022, pp. 20, 21, fig. 15.

26 Loomis and Loomis 1938, p. 97, fig. 237, and see now Stones 2013, cat. no. III–75, p. 362; although the casket's king lacks the beard of the Rylands Arthur, there are numerous examples elsewhere of Arthur represented as a younger king.

27 In Morrison and Hedeman 2010, p. 284. See Brieger 1957, pp. 149–50, for the pose as one of judgement.

28 Koechlin 1924, II, cat. no. 1290; the Cloisters panel is illustrated in Williamson and Davies 2014, pp. 654–55, fig. 2. The casket owes its name to the fact that it was presented at the Académie des Inscriptions et Belles-Lettres in Paris in 1745.

29 Gaborit-Chopin 2003, cat. no. 174.

30 Ibid., p. 418.

31 The fundamental surveys remain Bernheimer 1952, Hamburg 1963 and Husband 1980. For the Baird casket, Elżbieta Musialik has given a detailed and useful analysis of the wild man scenes and their cognates (Musialik 2022, pp. 16–23).

32 See Williamson 2019, cat. no. 103, and Rush 2024, pp. 246–54. Musialik has suggested that the wild men on the Baird casket might also be taken to symbolize Moors or Saracens, the intimidating enemies of Christians, and that the battles between them and the knights on the ivories perhaps represented the triumph of Christianity in a crusading context (Musialik 2024, pp. 328–31).

33 As recounted, for instance, in *The Knight of the Cart* (Lancelot), verses 5565–6056: Kibler 1991, pp. 276–81.

34 The identification of the figures as Tristan and Isolde was suggested by Paula Mae Carns to the anonymous writer of the catalogue entry for the 2021 auction, and repeated, with reservations, in Musialik 2022, p. 15.

35 Against this reading, perhaps, is the fact that she does not wear a crown.

36 This helmet and cloth plume match those on the mounted knight on the right side of the end panel, and might therefore be intended to show the same knight.

37 Knights and even dukes are shown in identical dress in the ivory casket with scenes from the story of the Châtelaine de Vergy of c. 1340 in the Musée du Louvre (Gaborit-Chopin 2003, cat. no. 175; É. Antoine in Morrison and Hedeman 2010, cat. no. 58).

38 A close inspection of the area around the figure's right wrist with ultra-violet light did not indicate that the hand had been broken off, and the brickwork above the wrist is untouched.

39 The head's presence is mysterious. It does not appear to play any part in the narrative, and is ignored by the flanking figures.

40 Musialik 2022, p. 13.

41 These are illustrations to the Merlin and Agravain stories (Sommer 1908–16, II, 394; V, 21; V, 135). I am most grateful to Alison Stones for her kind assistance in this matter, and for her valuable comments on other aspects of the casket.

42 A religious parallel could be drawn here with the apocryphal legend of Jephonias, a Jew who attempted to overturn the funeral bier of the Virgin and whose hands were cut off by the Archangel Michael, wielding a sword of fire; they were then miraculously restored on his embracing of Christianity (see Williamson and Davies 2014, cat. no. 284, p. 864, and James 1924, p. 208).

43 Morrison and Hedeman 2010, cat. no. 10.

44 Ibid., p. 121.

45 It may be relevant in this connection that the sword presented to Perceval by the Fisher King is also depicted lying

on a covered bier-like structure in an early fourteenth-century manuscript illumination of the Grail Procession in the Morgan Library and Museum in New York (Meuwese 2008a, figs 1–2; for the textual source, see Kibler 1991, pp. 419–20).

46 See the pertinent remarks in this connection by Barbara Newman in Newman 2016, pp. 60–65, and the useful survey in Meuwese 2008a.

47 See, for instance, the views of Richard H. Randall in Barnet 1997, pp. 63–79, 245–58 (1330–50); Paula Mae Carns 2005 (1330–50); Élisabeth Antoine in Morrison and Hedeman 2010, cat. nos. 55 (c. 1310–30) and 56 (c. 1300–20); Glyn Davies in Williamson and Davies 2014, pp. 654–59 (1320–30); Benedetta Chiesi in Ciseri 2018, pp. 282–86 (c. 1325–50); the present author in Williamson 2024, p. 11 (1310–30).

48 Antoine-König 2017, esp. pp. 161–62.

49 'Le travail est en relief peu accentué. Le style, parfois un peu sommaire et rapide, est vif et narratif. Bien différent de celui, souple et doux, des premières décennies du siècle, il correspond au courant des années 1330–1350, que l'on observe aussi sur certains coffrets de "la châtelaine de Vergy"; il est aussi très proche de celui des tablettes profanes du trésor de la cathédrale de Namur' (Gaborit-Chopin 2003, p. 418). There is the possibility that the casket from which the ivory panels came is not in fact of Parisian origin, but is a regional variation, and this may be germane to the place of production of the Baird casket.

50 Williamson and Davies 2014, cat. no. 126.

51 Gaborit-Chopin 2011 provides a thought-provoking summary of some of the problems.

52 Musialik 2022, p. 27.

53 Meuwese 2008, pp. 121–26; the quote is that of Élisabeth Antoine in Morrison and Hedeman 2010, p. 288. See also Gaborit-Chopin 2003, cat. no. 132.

54 Williamson 2024, p. 26. For ownership of the composite caskets, see also Musialik 2024, pp. 318–20.

55 The classic account of the subject to be found in Loomis and Loomis 1938 is still of fundamental value, even if dated in places and superseded by later studies; in this regard, see Stones 1991.

56 Stones 2013, cat. no. III–75, esp. pp. 364–66.

57 Even if the casket had been acquired in the region of Besançon, where both Andrew and Thomas Baird spent many years, it seems certain that it had been in Flanders at an earlier date because of the fifteenth-century restorations.

58 Koechlin 1924, cat. no. 1293 (Boulogne); the 'Lord Gort' casket has been published in Ross 1948, Bugslag 2007 and Carns 2011, but its authenticity has been doubted by Élisabeth Antoine, in Morrison and Hedeman 2010, p. 283, n. 1.

59 Williamson 2019, cat. no. 112.

60 'DIT GAF DONAE(s) / DE MOER JO(nc) VRAUE / TA(dria)NE TVOS INT JAER MCCCCLXXVIII'; Williamson 2019, p. 227, fig. 2 on p. 228.

61 Ibid., pp. 227–29.

62 Williamson and Davies 2014, pp. 483, 655, cat. nos. 233–38.

63 For the apposite case of the holdings of raw material in a Parisian sixteenth-century ivory workshop, see Baker 2023, pp. 71–77.

BIBLIOGRAPHY

ANTOINE-KÖNIG 2017
Antoine-König, É., 'The Return of Gawain:
Thoughts on Composite Caskets in the
Light of Some Recent Acquisitions', in
Davies and Townsend 2017, pp. 152–62

BAKER 2023
Baker, K., *A Merchant of Ivory in
16th-Century Paris: The Estate Inventory
of Chicart Bailly* (Leiden, 2023)

BARNET 1997
Barnet, P. (ed.), *Images in Ivory: Precious
Objects of the Gothic Age*, exh. cat., Detroit
Institute of Arts and Walters Art Gallery,
Baltimore (Princeton, 1997)

BERNHEIMER 1952
Bernheimer, R., *Wild Men in the Middle
Ages: A Study in Art, Sentiment, and
Demonology* (Cambridge, Mass., 1952)

BRIEGER 1957
Brieger, P., *English Art 1216–1307* (Oxford
History of English Art, IV) (Oxford, 1957)

BUGSLAG 2007
Bugslag, J., 'A "Lost" Ivory Casket in
the Gort Collection at the Winnipeg Art
Gallery', *RACAR*, 32 (2007), pp. 5–18

BULLOCH 1934
Bulloch, J.M., *The Bairds of Auchmedden
and Strichen, Aberdeenshire* (Peterhead,
1934)

CARNS 2005
Carns, P.M., '*Compilatio* in Ivory: The
Composite Casket in the Metropolitan
Museum', *Gesta*, 44/2 (2005), pp. 69–88

CARNS 2011
Carns, P.M., 'A Curious Collection in Ivory:
the Lord Gort Casket', in K. Fresco and A.D.
Hedeman (eds.), *Collections in Context: The
Organization of Knowledge and Community
in Europe* (Columbus, Ohio, 2011), pp.
246–74

CISERI 2018
Ciseri, I. (ed.), *Gli Avori del Museo
Nazionale del Bargello* (Milan, 2018)

DAVIES 2017
Davies, G., 'Francis Douce, FSA (1757–1834):
Scholar and Collector of Gothic Ivory
Carvings', in Davies and Townsend 2017,
pp. 246–54

DAVIES AND TOWNSEND 2017
Davies, G., and E. Townsend (eds.),
*A Reservoir of Ideas: Essays in Honour of
Paul Williamson* (London, 2017)

FRASER 1857
Fraser, W.N. (ed.), *Account of the Surname
of Baird, particularly of the families of
Auchmedden, Newbyth and Sauchtonhall*
(Edinburgh, 1857)

GABORIT-CHOPIN 2003
Gaborit-Chopin, D., *Ivoires médiévaux
Ve–XVe siècle*, Musée du Louvre, Paris,
Département des Objets d'Art (Paris, 2003)

GABORIT-CHOPIN 2011
Gaborit-Chopin, D., 'Gothic Ivories:
realities and prospects', in C. Hourihane
(ed.), *Gothic Art and Thought in the
Later Medieval Period. Essays in Honor of
Willibald Sauerländer* (Princeton, 2011),
pp. 157–75

HAMBURG 1963
Die wilden Leute des Mittelalters, exh. cat.,
Museum für Kunst und Gewerbe Hamburg
(Hamburg, 1963)

HUSBAND 1980
Husband, T., with the assistance of
G. Gilmore-House, *The Wild Man:
Medieval Myth and Symbolism*, exh. cat.,
Metropolitan Museum of Art (New York,
1980)

JAMES 1924
James, M.R. (trans.), *The Apocryphal New
Testament* (Oxford, 1924)

KIBLER 1991
Kibler, W.W. (trans.), *Chrétien de Troyes, Arthurian Romances* (London, 1991)

KOECHLIN 1911
Koechlin, R., 'Quelques ivoires gothiques français connus antérieurement au XIXe siècle', *Revue de l'art chrétien*, 61 (1911), pp. 281–92, 387–402

KOECHLIN 1924
Koechlin, R., *Les ivoires gothiques français*, 3 vols (Paris, 1924; repr. Paris, 1968)

LOOMIS AND LOOMIS 1938
Loomis, R.S., and L.H. Loomis, *Arthurian Legends in Medieval Art* (London and New York, 1938)

MCLAREN YOUNG 1947
McLaren Young, A., 'A French medieval ivory casket at the Barber Institute of Fine Arts', *Connoisseur*, 120 (1947), pp. 16–21

MEUWESE 2008
Meuwese, M., 'Chrétien in Ivory', *Arthurian Literature*, 25 (2008), pp. 119–52

MEUWESE 2008a
Meuwese, M.L., 'The Shape of the Grail in Medieval Art', in N.J. Lacy (ed.), *The Grail, the Quest, and the World of King Arthur* (Woodbridge, 2008), pp. 13–27

MORRISON AND HEDEMAN 2010
Morrison, E., and A.D. Hedeman (eds.), *Imagining the Past in France: History in Manuscript Painting, 1250–1500*, exh. cat., J. Paul Getty Museum (Los Angeles, 2010)

MUSIALIK 2022
Musialik, E., 'A 14th-century ivory casket with scenes from medieval romances: the newest addition to the so-called *coffrets composites* group', *Folia Historiae Artium*, new series, 20 (2022), pp. 9–28

MUSIALIK 2024
Musialik, E., 'Between Nostalgia and Reality. Chivalric ideals and their depiction during the reign of the last Capetians. The visual narration of the *coffrets composites* group', in Studer-Karlen 2024, pp. 313–43

NEWMAN 2016
Newman, B., 'Sacred, Secular, and Sensual: Three Case Studies in Late Medieval Crossover', in M. Bagnoli (ed.), *A Feast for the Senses: Art and Experience in Medieval Europe*, exh. cat., Walters Art Museum, Baltimore (Baltimore, 2016), pp. 55–73

ROSS 1948
Ross, D.J.A., 'Allegory and Romance on a Mediaeval French Marriage Casket', *Journal of the Warburg and Courtauld Institutes*, 11 (1948), pp. 112–42

RUSH 2024
Rush, K., 'Christian conscience in crisis. Visualising morality immorality on Gothic ivory caskets', in Studer-Karlen 2024, pp. 243–61

SOMMER 1908–16
Sommer, H.O., *The Vulgate Version of the Arthurian Romances, edited from manuscripts in the British Museum*, 8 vols. (Washington, 1908–16)

STONES 1991
Stones, A., 'Arthurian Art since Loomis', in *Arturus Rex II: Acta Conventus Lovainiensis 1987* (Leuven, 1991), pp. 21–78

STONES 2013
Stones, A., *Gothic Manuscripts 1260–1320, Part One* (A Survey of Manuscripts Illuminated in France), 2 vols. (London and Turnhout, 2013)

STUDER-KARLEN 2024
Studer-Karlen, M. (ed.), with the collaboration of Stefanie Agoues-Drabert, *Gothic Ivories between Luxury and Crisis* (Basel, 2024)

WILLIAMSON 2019
Williamson, P., *The Wyvern Collection: Medieval and Later Ivory Carvings and Small Sculpture* (London, 2019)

WILLIAMSON 2024
Williamson, P., 'Introduction', in Studer-Karlen 2024, pp. 9–32

WILLIAMSON AND DAVIES 2014
Williamson, P., and G. Davies, *Medieval Ivory Carvings 1200–1550*, Victoria and Albert Museum, 2 vols. (London, 2014)

First published in 2025

ISBN 978-1-915401-18-2

British Library Catalogue in Publishing Data

A CIP record of this publication is available from the British Library

Produced by Ad Ilissvm, an imprint of
Paul Holberton Publishing
paulholberton.com

Designed by Laura Parker

Distributed by Yale University Press, New Haven and London

Authorized Representative in the EU: Easy Access System Europe,
Mustam.e tee 50, 10621 Tallinn, Estonia, gpsr.requests@easproject.com

Printed by 4-Flying Srl trading as e-Graphic, Verona, Italy

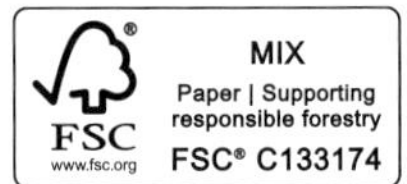

PHOTO CREDITS